Book of the Veil

By Peter Paddon

CAPALL BANN PUBLISHING

Book of the Veil

ISBN 1 898307 38 5

Also by Peter Paddon:

Through The Veil
Beyond the Veil

Cover design by Daryth Bastin
Cover and internal illustrations by Emma McKee

Published by:

Capall Bann Publishing
Freshfields
Chieveley
Berks
RG16 8TF

Acknowledgements

I would like to thank the following for their assistance in the writing of this book.

First and foremost, I would like to thank my wife Jackie, for putting up with the grumpy solitude I insist on when writing.

A special thank you goes to Thomas Toland who by "cracking the whip" at me whenever I thought of stopping, and by helping me to improve my writing style, has contributed as much to the books as I have myself.

To Emma McKee, for her artwork, I give my thanks and admiration.

And finally, to Olivia Robertson and the late Lawrence Durdin-Robertson (founders of the Fellowship of Isis), thank you for your support.

This book is dedicated with love and respect to Lawrence, 21st Baron Strathloch.

Table of Contents

FOREWORD

All sincere students of the religion of Ancient Egypt are
advised to study and to enjoy this rare and excellent
exposition of that unique faith. The author's style is clear
and, because he knows his subject so well, he makes even
the exceedingly complicated pattern of religious life in Egypt
easy to understand. Definition is needed for any follower of
the Egyptian occult practices ad this book provides the
essential information without which the seeker may become
lost in fantasy. Peter Paddon emphasises the earthly,
intelligent and practical characteristics of the ancient
Egyptian people, their enjoyment of life, their choice
blending of religion, magic and the supernatural with their
everyday way of living.

The scope of the book is wide. Particularly attractive is the
recounting of the Egyptian Creation myth, so that it has
spiritual relevance to modern seekers after the Mysteries.
What will attract occultists is his relatively unknown
information of the Egyptian Qabalah, which he describes as
"an acknowledged, but hitherto unexplored portion of the
Egyptian Mysteries", entitled "The Book of Gates" and its
subsequent development into the "Emissions of God".

As Director of Studies of the Thoth-Hermes Lodge of the
Sacred Hermetic Order of Asar-Ra, the author is in a strong
position to provide detailed and practical guidance on
creating a sacred space, casting an Egyptian circle, practice
of Egyptian magic and the design and consecration of
lamens. Above all Peter Paddon, Priest Hierophant of the
College of Isis, of the Fellowship of Isis, believes in the
Deities of Ancient Egypt and so is able to offer guidance and

1

spiritual inspiration to aid a candidate's communion with them. This can only come from an initiate of the Egyptian Mysteries. For though the author has the intellectual knowledge and ability to communicate teachings, he also has the one essential asset needed to help the reader share his experiences: he himself both knows that the Goddesses and Gods exist and loves them. Hence he is qualified to share mind and heart with the reader.

Olivia Robertson, Arch Priestess
Co-Founder of the Fellowship of Isis

INTRODUCTION

There are many paths to enlightenment and the Egyptian Mystery School is only one of them: but for many seekers after knowledge, it holds more fascination and glamour than any other classical Mystery. Even among followers of the modern Mystery movements such as neopagans and Wiccans, you will find many who are drawn to the lore of Ancient Egypt while still committed to their current path. Indeed I, my wife and several of our students all walk quite happily along both of these paths with no difficulty, and consider our lives the richer for it.

Nowadays there are shops devoted to the sale of books on the New Age, the Occult and related subjects. Walk into any one of these and you are bound to see a few books on Egyptian Magic. So why write another? Well, my aims are different. I have written this book with the intention of providing a sort of map, with directions on how to go about encountering the archetypes (gods, neters, whatever you wish to call them) at a personal level, for it is only at this level that we can truly comprehend their message.

Many have seen the ancient Egyptians as a race obsessed with death. It is true that they did spend much of their lives preparing for this event, but they were also a joyous race and lived their lives to the full. Their faith in their gods and in their priesthood (of both sexes) turned death from something to be feared and dreaded into something to be planned for and welcomed in its season, a transition to a new existence, and the lives of the people on earth were filled with humour and creativity.

In this book I provide a personal view of the deities of Khem, and give practical advice on encountering them. Although my work is based on my training within S.H.O.A.R., I must stress that everything given here is my own subjective belief - I am no great Egyptologist, nor do I claim any authority as a teacher other than that derived from the evident satisfaction of my own students. Although my research has taken place mostly within my own library and within the far reaches of my mind, I am no armchair mystic. Every single exercise I recommend, every attribute I describe, I have experienced for myself. Whether you encounter the gods of Egypt in your own home, in a quiet wood, or in one of the ancient Temples in Egypt, you will be moved by the experience. I have done all three, and in doing so my love for the gods and goddesses you will meet in these pages has grown beyond measure.

Do not expect me to disclose any great secrets within the words of this book. Those secrets are there, but you must use this book as a set of keys to the hidden depths of your innermost being in order to find them. That is why I have written this book, and if it helps you to learn one true thing about yourself, then my effort has been rewarded. Someone somewhere is bound to disagree with some of the things I say: good luck to them. All that I ask of you, the reader, is that you reserve judgement until you have experienced things for yourself. I say such-and-such is so because it works that way for me: don't dismiss it until you have tried to see if it works for you. If it doesn't, then try another way - we are all individuals, and all have our own personal path to walk.

Above all, I want you to enjoy this book, because life is about two things; learning and enjoying. If you have one without the other you are wasting your life, but the two combined make for true wisdom. Have fun, and open your eyes to the beauty of this world. For all its environmental crises and catastrophes; for all the politics and wars; for all the downright stupidity of man, it is still a wonderful place. Don't ever give up hope, because man IS becoming more spiritual, more attuned to the Earth. But it takes time and effort - and if we assume the worst then we have lost the fight before it has even begun.

Well, with my soapbox session over, take your first step on my guided tour of the universe according to the Priesthood of Khem. Look, learn, and have fun. If you like the book, let me know. If you don't like it, tell me why. Share your experiences with me, and we can all learn together.

Finally, remember that the only things that can limit your experience or your ability are the constraints of your own mind. Anything you can imagine is possible, and the human imagination has no limits!

1. THE LAND OF KHEM

Nowhere else on the face of our planet is there anywhere like Egypt. The Nile Valley is a world apart, a sealed valley about ninety-five miles wide and almost five hundred miles long, bordered on each side by vertical cliffs up to five hundred feet high and bounded by the deep desert. This unique environment led the Egyptians to be an inward looking race, with little concerns for the affairs of other countries, except for trade agreements and occasional border skirmishes. To the Ancient Egyptians, Egypt was the whole world.

For the Egyptian peasantry life was uncomplicated. During most of the year they worked in the fields, and during the three months of the year when the fertile flatlands were flooded by the Nile they worked on vast monuments of stone, temples and tombs that have made Egypt the marvel of the world ever since. Despite claims by some authors that these edifices were built by slave labour, all evidence points to a workforce that were not only happy with their lot, but actually proud of their work. This is simply because the whole idea of huge monuments started as an exercise in civil welfare, enabling the peasants to earn a living while their fields were unworkable.

But it was this very flooding of the Nile that made the valley fertile - so fertile, in fact, that there were two harvests each year. When the floodwaters receded the land was covered with the rich black soil that gave the land its name; Khemi, the Black Land. Agriculture was the established way of life, but the abundance of game made hunting a major past-time for nobles and farmers alike. Children ran naked in the heat, and adults wore light kilts or robes, with differentiation between classes being shown mainly by the decorations and jewellery that they wore.

The main social classes were the peasantry, the landowning peasantry, the gentry and the nobility. Starting from the bottom, the peasantry were a mobile workforce which went wherever it was needed. These people owned no land, and accommodation was normally provided for them by their employer for as long as their employment lasted. Their employers were the gentry, who appointed some of the more capable peasants to supervise work in the fields - to these they awarded small areas of land as an incentive to stay in the area. The gentry inherited or were awarded their land, and paid taxes and tithes to the state.

Unlike social classes in other civilisations, it was possible for an individual to rise through the classes on the merit of their abilities. A good example of this was Horemheb, who began life as a peasant and ended as vizier to Queen Hapshepsut, a rank roughly equivalent to Prime Minister. The gentry were therefore always seeking to do their very best in the hope that they might one day be awarded an office in the Temple or Palace and thus rise to the station of Noble.

The nobles owned larger estates but were freed from the onus of running them by appointing overseers, leaving them free to attend to their higher duties. Egypt was a hugely wealthy country where gold was plentiful, and to be a noble in that age was to live a life of luxury and privilege. There were many social events and religious festivals to participate in, as well as everything from competitive sports to skilled pastimes, such as hunting and fishing.

The priesthood were a class apart. Consisting of both male and female initiates, and regarded with reverence and awe by the populace, they were totally integrated with and yet somehow beyond the rest of society. There were four grades of priesthood. The Uab, or We'eb, was an unspecialised low level initiate, who learnt by observing the daily patterns of the temple and saw to all the mundane chores. One of the only ritual acts they were permitted to perform was the libation, which meant carrying great heavy offering vessels out of the temple and pouring their contents back to the earth. Indeed, the term We'eb means "libator" and "empty vessel", referring to the fact that the uab could only offer him/herself as such to the gods in the hope of being filled with knowledge.

The next grade of priesthood were more important. Called Hem Neters, meaning "servants of the God", they were actively taught the outer Mysteries and trained in specialised areas. They would become scribes, specialists in ritual, healers, or astrologers. They assisted in the Temple rituals, and would receive the offerings of the people in the outer court.

Next came the Hem Neter Tepy, or First Servant of the God, of which each temple would have only a few. They acted as High Priests and High Priestesses for the rituals, and acted for the Pharaoh in the daily rituals. The members of this third grade were all members of an inner organisation, called the Four Orders. From the 12th Dynasty this had its headquarters at Abydos, and there its members would congregate to perform the rites of the Inner Mysteries. The most senior among the Hem Neter Tepys were initiated into the fourth grade and became Kher Heb priests. These performed the most sacred rites, administered to the spiritual needs of the Pharaoh himself, and performed a ceremony called the Opening of the Mouth (used to breathe spiritual life into something) on statues, temples, and the dead body of the Pharaoh as part of the funeral rites. These priests had phenomenal magical power, and were said to be able to replace severed heads, cause waters to change their course, and turn staffs into serpents. Scholars from all over the classical world came to Egypt to study from these initiates.

The Egyptian Priesthood were neither celibate nor ascetic, believing in a policy of moderation in all things: they saw self-denial as an extreme to be avoided just as much as over-indulgence. They married (one wife) and had children, drank wine in moderation, ate balanced diets which included white meats (and a lot of onions!), and maintained high standards of personal hygiene. The temples had sacred lakes in which the initiates bathed prior to every rite - and there were at least three each day. They shaved their heads because they could not keep their hair clean in the dusty environment, and rubbed scented oils on their bodies so that they were pleasing to their god.

You have probably read or been told that the people of the Land of Khem indulged in perversions and strange sexual practices. This is mostly untrue: they had a healthy and open attitude to sex, but were rarely licentious. Homosexuality was a crime, even though it was sometimes indulged in by young nobles of the late period as a statement of mastery over their siblings, like the archetypal private school bully of today. Even the famous incestuous marriages of royalty were far less scandalous than some make out: although incest was lawful in Egypt it was frowned upon just as much as in modern times. Yes, new pharaohs would marry a sister, mother, or aunt - but there was a very good reason for this.

Although the Pharaoh was the active ruler of Egypt, his son would not automatically rule after him. The right to rule was passed through the matriarchal line - in other words, the husband of his daughter or widow would become the new

Pharaoh. Therefore, a marriage of convenience was needed to legitimise the new Pharaoh. A common arrangement would be for the new Pharaoh to marry other wives while his sister-Queen was given apartments where she could (discreetly!) entertain her own lover. There were a few instances of the marriage between a Pharaoh and his sister, mother, or (in the case of Akhenaton) daughters becoming a sexual union, but this always resulted in a rapid loss of respect from the people. Pharaohs who broke this unwritten rule tended not to last long.

The reason the right to rule passed through the Queen was simple. The Queen was always the High Priestess of the Mysteries, trained from birth in the secrets of the Inner Temple. She chose her husband, under advice of the Four Orders. Thus it was the Four Orders who truly controlled Egypt, since they could choose to overlook an apparent heir who seemed unsuitable and choose a younger brother, a cousin, or even a non-related prince in his stead. This custom continued until the Greeks began the process of separating the Temple from the State.

It was this process, continued by the Romans, that led to Egypt slipping into anonymity, although it was the Coptic Christians who dealt the Temples the death blow, desecrating buildings and statues. From then on, worship of the old Gods moved from the temples into the home, until the Muslim invasion of Egypt in the mid seventh century AD. The Muslims banned the ancient language of Khem, and by that simple act separated the Gods from their people. Without its language, Egypt became just another arab state. Luckily, much of the sacred wisdom had been placed in the cultures of other lands, such as the Greek Mysteries, the Hebrew Hekalot teachings, and even (according to some Greek texts) the British Druidic system.

Over the centuries, the physical remains of Egypt have been studied, and the spiritual essence of Khem has from time to time been tapped. Now, as what little there is of the written Mysteries of Khem becomes available in translation, we are finally able to piece together more and more areas of the Mysteries by a process of academic research and mystical insight. One such area to come to light is included in this book. Just as modern-day schoolchildren delight in the use of puns to refer to obscene or ridiculous subjects, so the initiates of Khem used puns to hide their esoteric secrets from the uninitiated. The priests used this technique to evolve the concept of the "Emissions of the God", explained in a later chapter.

There are many examples of this technique known to scholars, but despite this it is ignored, or mentioned in passing without any attempt to use it in the way it was intended. Perhaps the most obvious example is the word Nemmes, which is usually taken as the name of the cloth or leather headdress that almost symbolises Ancient Egypt. But this word has another meaning which explains why the garment was so appropriate for initiates: the word Nemmes is also the verb "to enlighten". A more esoteric example is the Egyptian name for Anubis, Anpu. It also means Prince (Anubis, as Son of Osiris, is Prince of the Underworld) and is the verb "to wrap or swathe", which could not be more apt for the god of embalming!

Brief examinations of some other deities show similarly appropriate meanings. Asar, the non-Hellenised version of Osiris, means "to travel", "to introduce", "tamarisk tree", "foliage", and "retribution", all parts of the legend of Osiris. Aset - Isis - means "one who laments", and "chest" or "coffer", which fits what we know about Isis quite nicely. It would be useful to examine all of the deities in this fashion, but space within this volume is too limited for that.

The esoteric use of the pun puts a whole new slant on our perspective on Ancient Egypt. For instance, one might wonder why such a fuss was made when "one of the Pharaoh's trees was cut down". But if you realise that the word for tree, djed, also means "column", "pillar", or "support" then you can see - what the passage means is that one of the Pharaoh's supporters has been killed! The Egyptians spoke in pictures and ideas as much as in concrete terms. A library becomes "a papyrus swamp". A dead person is "under the sand". Once you learn how to think like an Egyptian, a whole new world of meaning for hitherto nonsense passages opens up.

Spell 397 in the Coffin Texts, verses 115 and 116 - quoted at the start of the chapter on Egyptian Qabalah - contains a magical method of counting that makes full use of the technique of puns, and turns out to be of much greater significance that it at first appears. In this text, the magician before being carried across the spiritual Nile by the Ferryman is asked to prove his wisdom, and to show his ability to "count on his fingers". As Jacq says in his book "Egyptian Magic";

> *"Each finger, each numerical act, has a deep meaning. [This very detailed counting demands long study. In our opinion, it is the origin, not yet recognised, of the numerical Kabbala.] This is not a question of ordinary mental arithmetic, but of the creation of the world by Numbers."*

As you will see in the chapter on the Egyptian Qabalah, I am in agreement with Jacq's statement and have begun to study this text deeply. This is perhaps one of the most important areas of esoteric research into the Egyptian Mysteries, for a clearly defined correlation between the Temples of the Nile and the Upper Room of the Qabalist can only serve to unite western mystics more closely and be of benefit to everybody. It is not necessary to see one as being derived from the other, but merely to accept that they have a common source, be that divine or mundane. Whatever the reason, they are directly linked, and recognition of this fact can surely only lead to a better understanding of both systems.

2. CREATION

The Ancient Egyptian peasantry were a very simple people, and thought in very basic terms. This made it necessary for each temple to present to those under its care a straightforward creation legend composed of easily grasped images, with the god of that particular temple at its heart. To us, this makes it look as if there are many different and seemingly conflicting versions. For the inner priesthood, however, the god of creation was Atum. According to the scriptures of Memphis, Atum is self-created, and brought the universe into existence with a single word, his true name. One scripture begins;

> *"Kheper-i kheper kheperu*
> *Kheper-kuy m kheperu*
> *m Khepri kheper m sep tepy..."*

This is equivalent to the beginning of Genesis, and can be translated as;

> *"Thus saith the Lord of All: when I became, the becoming became. I have become in becoming the form of Khepri who came into being on the First Time. When I became, the transformations became, all the metamorphoses coming to pass after I had become. I did all that I desired in this nonexistent world, and I dilated myself in it.....I contracted my own hand, all alone, before there was any birth. My own mouth came to me, and Magic was my name."*

The creation this fascinating scripture speaks of is not only that of the gods, but also of the universe. While the gods were expectorated (spat out), the universe was created out of the semen of Atum, brought forth by the act of masturbation. Atum is spoken of as uniting with the Nun (the Void) to form Atum-Nun, the cosmic Father-Mother of creation. Life itself, according to the Memphis scriptures, came from the heart and tongue of Atum.

The first gods to spring forth from Atum were Shu and Tefnut, who were the twin lion gods who guarded the entrance to the Kingdom of Osiris. Their wanderings brought the universe into manifestation, as they defined the six directions of physical space. Atum then manifested himself within his creation as the god Ra.

"Atum" means "totality" in a sense of being ultimately perfect and unchangeable. He is pictured as a man wearing the Double Crown of Upper and Lower Egypt. Secondary to his role as creator is a role rarely mentioned by the Egyptians, that of destroyer. In the "Book of the Dead", in a dialogue between himself and Osiris (who was his manifestation in the underworld), Atum states that he will eventually destroy the world, drowning gods, men, and the earth in the primal waters of the Nun. Only he and Osiris will live on, in the form of serpents.

Shu and Tefnut united to give birth to Geb and Nut (the Earth and Sky), who bore Osiris, Isis, Set, and Nephthys. The story of the birth of these, the children of Geb and Nut is interesting in itself.

Seeking to keep the beautiful Nut for himself, Ra had forbidden Geb and Nut to "embrace" each other, but by stealth they managed to do so. Eventually Ra discovered their secret, and cursed them that they would not bear a child in any month of the year. Geb and Nut fled to Thoth for help, and he took pity on them. Thoth was one of several

Star Gods who appear to have originated from outside Atum's creation, and he was the wily god of learning and science. He played a game of "counters" (a primitive form of draughts) with the Moon god, and won for Geb and Nut a seventy-second part of the Moon's light. With this he formed five new days. Because these days were outside the official Egyptian calendar of 360 days, Nut was able to give birth to her children during that time. An interesting detail from the legend is that although Osiris and Isis are said to be twins, this legend states that each of the five children were born on the five consecutive days. The legend says;

Upon the first of these new-made days Osiris was born, and a voice from heaven proclaimed, "the Lord of all things hath appeared". Upon the second of the five new days Horus the Elder was born. Upon the third, Set came into the world, being born neither at the proper time, nor by the right place, but by forcing his way through a wound in his mother's side. Upon the fourth day was born the Goddess Isis in the marshes of Lower Egypt. And upon the fifth and last day was born Nephthys.

The Egyptians believed that the Creator, Atum, formed himself out of the void or primal matter (the Nun), and then united with the void to form the universe and the gods. This is basically the same as the Qabalistic interpretation of Kether condensing out of Ain Soph Aur (the Limitless Light) which itself forms out of Ain Soph (without limit). Ain Soph ultimately derives from Ain (the Void, or Nothingness). If this Void of the Qabalah can be likened to the Nun, then Atum is Ain Soph, without limit. This can be explained by the fact that the Creator existed before Time and Space, so there was nothing to limit him - the Void and himself was all there was. The Limitless Light then becomes his spittle, his semen, and his word, that is, his creative impulse.

Let us look at this from a different viewpoint. One theory of Quantum physics states that the universe was formed by the action of a self-formed point of matter with a false vacuum. Before we go into how it happened, let us examine the two "participants" more closely.

It has been discovered that the smaller subatomic particles - electrons and smaller - can move between points in zero time. This has been explained by the theory of spontaneous generation, which states that the smaller an object is, the less energy is required for its formation. This means that if something is small enough, it will take no energy at all to form.

A false vacuum is one of several types of vacuum that have been found to exist. It is the same as a normal vacuum until you try to destroy it by removing it, when a great deal of energy is produced. The theory of creation is that in the void of nothingness, no-space, no-time, that preceded the universe, subatomic particles were continually spontaneously forming and unforming, until circumstances arose involving a false vacuum. Once these circumstances changed and the false vacuum collapsed, it released the energy that formed the whole of creation - the Big Bang! The similarities between this, the Qabalah, and the Egyptian legend are too great to be ignored.

Another interesting parallel between the legend and modern science is the calling into being of the gods of creation themselves. According to one version, the semen from the Creator's ejaculation formed into nine gods; four pairs, and the Creator as a manifest being. Through the electron microscope, the human sperm can be seen to be composed of eight paired filaments around a central core, and therefore consisting of nine parts.

On a superficial level, then, the creation legend of Ancient Egypt can be said to derive from true knowledge of the creative forces involved - both on a human and on a universal level. Looking deeper leads us to recognise the gods as metaphors for the creative forces that govern existence - a way of presenting these forces in a form that ordinary people can accept and work with. All schools of the occult, be they western or oriental, Pagan or Christian, have a hierarchy of beings that are considered to be elements of a greater whole that cannot itself be comprehended by man - it is simply too immense for mere mortals to envisage Indeed, one legend has it that of all the gods, only Thoth the Wise could comprehend the nature of the Creator.

The Egyptians seem to have gone to great lengths to group their deities together in pairs. Of course nobody can be certain of their reasons for doing so, but several theories spring to mind. There seem to be two types of pairs in the system; opposites and complementaries. A case of opposites is the traditional pairing of Set and Nephthys as husband and wife. While the God of Storms and the Desert would not be expected to rest easily with the goddess of motherly love and protection, but this is the case. This is because this pair of opposites shows that the way to balance the fiery emotions is with the calming effect of love and patience. Pairs of gods who complement each other, such as Osiris and Isis, represent the active and passive aspects of the same characteristic. Osiris, as the god of the harvest and agricultural science, represents the physical side of working with nature, whereas Isis as the goddess of natural magic represents the intuitive or spiritual side. This shows the active and passive aspects of the same force.

Pairings resulting in offspring are a further confirmation of this theory. The uniting of Osiris and Isis brought forth Horus, who is a manifestation of the archetypal Saviour of all religions. This archetype occurs as the avenging warrior, son of the slain god, or as the resurrected form of the slain god. God of Fire, father of the Lords of the Four Quarters, he is the Solar Logos, the embodiment of knowledge and power, the perfection of imperfect Man. Isis and Osiris can be seen here as physical man and spiritual man: only when the two are successfully integrated can we attain the state of Horus - perfected man.

The secondary role of Atum as destroyer is also mirrored in many religions. Shiva and Shakti both have their destroyer aspects, and a much quoted Christian phrase, "the Lord giveth and the Lord taketh away", implies that Jehovah is as much the god of death as he is of life.

Many scholars have explained the pairing of attributes and of the gods themselves as being the result of Egypt being the amalgamation of two countries, and also due to the influence of the Nile, which splits Egypt along its length. If that were the sole explanation, though, it would not explain the essential dualism of every religion. All pantheons consist of male and female deities, and most consider their ultimate god to be hermaphrodite, ie., both sexes. For the Tantric adept, the goal is the permanent union of Shiva and Shakti in a formless ecstasy, while for the Egyptians the source of all was Atum-Nun, the eternal Father-Mother. For the Qabalist and western magician, the final goal is to unite with Ain Soph Aur, and free oneself from the fetters of polarity and form - in Egyptian terminology, to become a Khu, one with Atum.

The destruction of all save Atum and Osiris can be viewed in several ways. On a mundane level, the significance of this legend applies to the development of the Mysteries, for after the destruction of the land of Khem (Ancient Egypt) by the Greeks, Romans and then the Arabs, the only Orders to survive were those of Ra and Osiris, their wisdom (serpents) being largely saved whilst those of others was wholly lost. These two orders grouped together under the banner of the Mysteries of Isis, and spread throughout the civilised world.

Another way of looking at it is this; mystics and magicians seek to break the fetters of reincarnation, space and time, and attain unity with the Nun in order to pass to a higher state of existence. The Void itself is not an acceptable target, because the human mind cannot normally cope with the concept of its own disintegration, and so we may take our target as Atum, the Creator. Likewise, Osiris symbolises the path of spiritual perfection whereby we may reach that target. An analogy may be drawn with the reported words of Jesus; "I am the Way, the Truth, and the Light. No man cometh unto the Father but by me". In other words, this destruction will occur personally for each one of us, and represents our passage from this existence to the next - our passage through the Veil.

3. OSIRIS

Osiris is perhaps best known as the God of the Underworld. Originally called Asar, his name derives from the word "Woser", meaning "The Mighty One". In his legend Osiris was depicted as King of Egypt, and was credited with bringing civilisation to the country;

> *"Osiris, being now King of Egypt, applied himself towards civilising his countrymen, by turning them from their former indigent and barbarous course of life; he moreover taught them how to cultivate and improve the fruits of the earth; he gave them a body of laws to regulate their conduct by, and instructed them in that reverence which they should pay to the gods."*

Osiris travelled round the world, inducing all that he met to follow his example, conveying his reasoning by way of music and songs. While he was away, his brother Set constantly strove to introduce his own ideas into the governing of the land: only the power of Isis, the wife of Osiris, was able to keep Set's chaotic influence in check. By the time Osiris returned, Set had gathered about him seventy-two conspirators, and had formed a plan to seize the throne.

Set had his artificers make a beautifully decorated and valuable chest, designed to fit exactly around the body of Osiris. At the great banquet held to celebrate the return of Osiris to Egypt, Set brought out the marvellous chest, and offered it as a gift to anyone who could fit into it exactly. Everyone tried it, but of course it would only fit Osiris, who was last to try it. As he laid down in it, Set and his henchmen slammed the lid down, and nailed it shut. Not

Osirus

content with this, they then sealed it with molten lead, and threw it into the sea at the mouth of the Nile. This happened on the 17th day of the month Aethyr, with the Sun in Scorpio, when Osiris was twenty-eight years old.

Isis searched long and hard for the chest, and when she eventually found it she took it to a secluded place, where she use her magic to unite with her dead husband, resulting in the birth of a son, Horus. The chest containing the body of Osiris was hidden, but Set discovered it, and tore the body into fourteen pieces, which he scattered throughout the land. Once again Isis was forced to journey in search of Osiris, and wherever she found a part of him, she set up a shrine in which she buried a replica. The real parts were put together and embalmed by Anubis, the god who guides the souls of the dead. Horus eventually grew up to avenge the death of his father, for which he was given the throne of Egypt, and to Osiris was given the throne of the Underworld.

The legend is sketchy at best, and many versions contradict each other, but the actual role of Osiris in the Mysteries is clear. Like all the gods, he had many titles which help one to understand his nature, but like many other major gods, he also acquired titles (which may be ignored for the moment) from the cult of local gods which were absorbed into the Osiris cult as it gained in size and popularity.

FOREMOST OF THE WESTERNERS refers to his importance as a funerary god, as the land of the dead was considered to be in the west.

HE WHO DWELLS IN HELIOPOLIS is a direct reference to his relationship to Ra and the Sun.

HE WHO DWELLS IN ORION WITH A SEASON IN THE SKY AND A SEASON ON EARTH connects Osiris with one of Egypt's most important constellations, and refers to his dual material and astral roles.

These are just a few of his many titles. Although he is commonly thought of as an agricultural god by those who study nature magic, his involvement with agriculture is actually quite small. It is however a natural progression from his position as the Lord of the Underworld, as which he was master of the cycles of life and death - including seed time and harvest.

His best known role is as Judge of the Dead, and as such he is described as the "Lord of Maat", and as being "United with Maat", meaning Lord of Truth. It is in this role that he is seen in his earliest appearance in the Egyptian scriptures - indeed, in the "Book of the Dead", the deceased is referred to as "Osiris the Scribe Ani", or whatever the name and occupation of the deceased was.

Many scholars credit Osiris with existence as a mortal king, and this is quite possible, as many races have deified great leaders. This is, however, irrelevant when considering the meaning of the legend. Whatever the origins, the legend of Osiris carries in it ancient man's explanation of the concept that Osiris stands for.

As I have previously stated, there is a great similarity between the Egyptian legends, scientific theory, and the Qabalah. Whilst my personal attribution of the gods on the Tree of Life may differ from that of others, it does give an insight into the inner meanings of the legends, and I therefore give it in full here.

1. KETHER. Ra, as a manifestation of Atum, is found in Kether. Its image is that of an ancient bearded king, and is referred to as the "Existence of Existences", the "Ancient of Ancients", and the "Primordial Point", among other titles.

2. CHOKMAH. Following on the path of the Tree and also next in the legends are Shu and Tefnut, in the Sphere known as the "Crown of Creation". This refers to more than the creation of the earth, as this Sphere is represented by the Zodiac.

3. BINAH. Geb and Nut fall naturally into this Sphere, called the "Creator of Faith". It is the "Foundation of Primordial Wisdom", a good title for the abode of the foundation (parents) of the gods of Knowledge and Wisdom.

4. CHESED. Also known as Gedulah, "the Glory", this is the sphere of Osiris and Isis, symbolised by a "Mighty crowned and throned King". This Sphere is said to contain all the Holy Powers, and from it emanate all spiritual virtues.

5. GEBURAH. Represented by the depiction of a mighty warrior in his chariot, the next Sphere is one of severity and strength. It houses Set and his wife Nephthys. The home of justice and fear, this "Sphere of the Vision of Power" contains energy and courage along with Set's best known trait of destruction.

6. TIPHARETH. Symbolised by a majestic king, a child, and a sacrificed god, this is the home of the Son, the Sun, and of devotion to the Great Work. This, the Sphere of Horus is the centre of a hexagram of powerful influences.

7. NETZACH. A beautiful naked woman represents this Sphere, where abides Hathor, Goddess of love, music and dance. Called the "Vision of Beauty Triumphant", this Sphere reminds us of Hathor's dual aspect - she is also the vengeful lioness, Sekhmet.

8. HOD. Thoth is at home here, in the "Vision of Splendour", and the "Perfect Intelligence". Thoth was called Mercury by the Greeks, and was also known as the Lord of the Secret Words and the Champion of Truthfulness.

9. YESOD. "The Foundation", the "Vision of the Machinery of the Universe". What better place to find Ptah, the Divine Architect of the Universe, who continues creation according to the Master Plan?

10. MALKUTH. Finally, Anubis guards the "Entrance to the Kingdom", the "Gate of Death", also known as the Gate of Tears, Justice, and of Prayer. This is the gateway to initiation.

From inspecting Chesed, we learn that it continues the work of organising and preserving "that which the All-Father has begotten" - so Osiris teaching civilisation to the people may be considered an action typical of the force represented by this sphere. In contrast to the warrior and war-like image of Set, Osiris is seen as the throned lawgiver, bringing order and improving and building upon what his people already possess. Man has a potent need for a framework of belief on which to build a growing awareness of unity with Atum: as an archetypal force, Osiris and Isis provide that framework.

Traditionally, the colour of Osiris is green or white - he is usually depicted as being covered in white mummy wrappings with a green face. The wrappings are obviously a representation of his role as god of the dead, and the green face can be seen as representing his nature aspect - Egypt's Green Man! The colour of Isis is blue, and this is the colour associated with Chesed, signifying that organisation is not enough, the wisdom of Isis is just as important - indeed, while Osiris was abroad exerting the influence of Order, it was Isis who was on the throne of Egypt.

Let us now look at the name of Osiris. We have seen how his original name, Asar, derived from the word Woser, the Mighty One, but let us look deeper. The word Osiris is of Greek origin, and numerically adds up to 120 in the new system, or 131 in the old Greek system. These add up to three, or four. Using the old system four represents "friendliness" to the Buddhist, God "the Farmer's Friend" to the Christian, and the "Vision of Love" to the Alchemist. It is symbolised by the wand, sceptre, or crook (traditionally Osiris carries all three). The figure relating to four is the pyramid that plays an important part in the cult of Osiris, and in the system of the Qlipphoth (the Dark Side of the Tree of Life) four is "The Breakers in Pieces", which is basically a good description of the fate of Osiris under the hands of Set.

Looking at the original word Asar, we get the number 77, which breaks down into 14 and then five. Five bears a direct relationship to Set, and 14 to Isis or Hathor. Seven doubled is a strong reinforcement of ultimate victory, the Occult Intelligence, the Messiah, and the Vision of Beauty Triumphant. Horus, the Son and avenger of Osiris, is traditionally placed in the Qabalistic sphere of Tiphareth, the Sphere of Beauty, and this could refer to his victory over Set, and his part in the legend as successor/reincarnation of Osiris.

Using the modern system, we get 35 (reduces to eight) and 12 (reduces to three). Using eight, we see the close relationship between Osiris and Thoth who in the legend helped Isis to conceive Horus by his secret knowledge. Also, the date of Osiris' death was the seventeenth, also adding up to eight, and showing the need for sacrifice. The three, giving the Vision of Sorrow, shows the companion of the sacrifice - it was through the grief of Isis, and her search for the body of Osiris that she came into magickal knowledge that ultimately enabled her to perform her miracles.

Now we shall look at Osiris from a numerological viewpoint. For simplicity, I am using only the modern form, the technique used is given in the appendices.

Osiris adds up to eight, giving a high regard for law and order, especially in areas relating to Tradition. In his heart, Osiris is a warrior, but suppresses this because of his powerful spiritual destiny. He has a strong mystical influence in his life, with much inner peace under his outward role of authority and rulership. A danger is indicated from a martial aspect of his life.

Osiris is usually depicted with several symbols, the crook, the flail, the Tet column, and the Atef Crown. These are all symbols that can be used to generate a link with him. The crook was a symbol of leadership in ancient times, and points to the royal origins of Osiris. But it is more than that. The crook is a model of the implement used to remove the brain of the dead body during mummification, so carrying it symbolises authority over the dead as much as over the living. As a shepherd's crook, it has all the usual connotations of guidance, protection, and leadership by example.

The flail is a symbol from the role of Osiris as god of agriculture. It was used in a practical way to separate the grain from the chaff, and was also used as a punishment by the overseer. In this way it became associated with judgement, and therefore also symbolises the judiciary role of Osiris.

The Tet is more complicated. Linked directly with the legend of the death of Osiris, various authorities differ in its exact interpretation. To some it is the backbone of Osiris, to some his phallus. Others see it in the Tamarisk tree that the sarcophagus was lodged in, and yet another group say that it represents the pillar of the King of Byblos in which Isis found the body of Osiris. Esoterically, all of these are to an extent correct. The Tet symbolises all of these things and more, because it is also the ladder that was shown to initiates to depict their journey to the stars.

The Atef crown is a symbol of divine royalty, and is composed of the White Crown of Egypt adorned with the twin plumes of Truth - the Double Maati, said to represent the divine protection of Isis and Nephthys - and the ram's horns attributed to a deity named Asar-Ra in the Inner Mysteries. When Osiris is depicted wearing this crown and the wrappings of a Mummy, and bearing the crook and flail, we see him as the All-Powerful Lord of Eternity, One with Ra.

But what is is like to work with Osiris? As one who has mediated for the god for many years, I experience his presence as that of a calm and wise man. Like many of the Egyptian deities, he maintains a certain distance which enables the mediator to function both as participant and observer. When he has been invoked, you feel the need to stand upright and regally, and your words are measured and carefully chosen. He is a good deity to invoke to aid in decision-making, and his power over matters of judgement is evident - but he will not save you from just punishment. His greatest practical use is to right a wrong, and esoterically he is a great teacher. Above all he is a gentle god, and I would recommend him as your first contact with the deities of Egypt.

Occasionally the experience of mediating Osiris can go beyond the mere invocation, and you can find yourself experiencing a transcendent vision. For many this is an initiatory event, and for all it is a life-changer. When Osiris is summoned, Isis is never far away, nor Ra or Horus, so rituals involving him always have an atmosphere of family. While you are under the protection of Osiris, no deity will deny a just request, but an unjust request will cause Osiris to depart.

PATHWORKING

Each of the chapters on the gods will have a section like this. It is a guided spiritual journey to encounter the deity in a way that will enhance your understanding of him or her. The journeys will have a spiritual effect on you that increases with each one you do. You can either do them in the order that they appear in the book, or follow the order of deities in the correspondence tables in appendix 3.

Although it is by no means essential to take protective measures when doing these exercises, you will find that visualising yourself surrounded by a circle or sphere of light prior to starting will enhance the experience.

You will need to prepare yourself for the journey. Ideally, have someone there to read the journey to you, or record it on cassette, and play it back to yourself. Seat yourself in a comfortable chair, and take a few moments to get as comfortable as you can. Try not to cross your legs or arms as this is a defensive posture that will lessen your concentration.

After you have taken a few deep breaths, and you feel really comfortable, begin your tape or get your partner to read the journey to you. At the end of the journey, have a good stretch and a hot drink - in Ancient Egypt it was traditional to drink hot chocolate after spiritual work. Now for the journey itself.

Visualise yourself in a corridor. The walls are of stone, and there are stone pillars along each side of the corridor. Walk forward, noticing as you do the pictures carved into the stone, of men and gods.

At the end of the corridor is a double door with two guardians. They are men, dressed in kilts, leather tunics, and sandals, bearing spears or staffs. As you approach, they bar your way with their weapons, but a voice from beyond the door commands them to let you enter.

They stand aside, pushing the doors open, and you pass through the portal into a large hall, long and high. On either side are men and women in rich robes and jewels, who stand silently, observing you as you walk towards the far end of the hall, where a flight of stone steps leads up to a throne.

As you get closer, you see a man seated upon the throne, wearing a white kilt, golden jewellery, and a flowing cloak of green. On his head, above a noble but gentle face, is a crown of white leather, the traditional white crown of Egypt. This particular crown, though, is decorated with an ostrich plume on either side, and in the centre of the man's brow is a pair of ram's horns extending sideways from the band of the crown.

Now you are close enough to see that he holds in his hands the Crook and Flail, and you realise that you are in the presence of Osiris. Walk to the foot of the steps, and look up at the King of the Underworld. He smiles at you, and gestures with the crook for you to come up to him, which you do.

Now for the first time you look into the eyes of Osiris, and see his compassion and love for mankind reflected there. Then you notice that something is odd about his face. Seeing your reaction, he signals a servant to draw near. The servant holds up a mirror in such a way that you look at your face in it as it is held next to the face of Osiris. You see that the two faces are identical.

Smiling, Osiris explains that you and he are one, for all who follow the path of wisdom are one, and he is merely man made perfect. He places his crook and flail on his knees and takes your hands, and you feel the energy and power of him flow through you.

"One day," he says, "you will enter my kingdom and remain, but for now must your visit be short. Depart from here, and take my blessing with you." With a last look, you turn and retrace your steps to the doorway, passing through and walking down the corridor. As you walk, everything fades, and you find yourself once more seated in your physical self, and you realise that the journey is over.

MEDITATION

1. Here are the words of A.F.N.A., High Priest of Osiris in the Land of Khem, maa Kheru, triumphant in Peace, un-Nefer, one with the Light.

2. Praise and songs of glory unto Thee, O Osiris, un-Nefer, Lord of the Hidden Place, whose form is majestic. Be Thou in my heart, O Bringer of Harvest, and inspire Thou me to write of Truth and Beauty in Thine honour.

3. Great is Thy form, and wise are Thy words, O Lord of the Two Rivers. Thy servant waiteth, and is but an empty vessel to be filled with Thy Luminescence. Breathe Thou into him that Divine Inspiration that causeth the Earth to rock on its foundations, O Thou who art Endless Light.

4. Thus saith the Lord of All: "I see thee in thy place far from this land, and I feel thy sincerity. Be thou now one with Me in thought and form, and let My thoughts be thine, for thou art truly a Khu in the eyes of the Gods, and for thee is a homestead beyond the Hall of the Double Maati. Write thou now of the things that thou dost see, and feel, and hear with thine inner senses.

5. Many are the prophets of my teachings in the Land of Khem, that great nation that exists only in the hearts of the initiates since its fall from prominence in the affairs of man. Of these, thou art one who has served well before, and so shalt thou do again."

6. Mine eyes are filled with a radiance like unto that of the Sun Disk in His journeys, and once more the sweet scents of the Temple are all around me. The fragrance of the Kyphi incense fills my nostrils and opens the subtle sense of my soul to the awareness of my unity with He Who Strides Across the Land in Glory.

7. I see the procession going forth from the Temple to greet Ra at His Rising, and hear the chants of the city dwellers in the dawning day. "Glory unto Thee, O Great Ra," I hear. "May Thy journey be swift and free from hindrance, and may Thy Right Eye shed forth rays of goodness upon us, and let Thy Left Eye strike down those who seek to hinder us."

8. Then do I hear the Voice of He who is Mighty in the Secret Words. "Do thou now set forth the secret of the sacred incense for thy followers, O thou who dost seek many answers. Fourteen ingredients shall thou take, and thou shalt mix them in accordance with the hidden name of the scent. Thou shalt take honey, and wine, and wood from the cedar tree, and mix them with the fragrance of the Wise Ones, of life and death, frankincense and myrrh. To this shalt thou add the gum of the acacia tree and the resin of ancient trees, amber. Fragrant rushes from the riverside shalt thou crush and mix in with hot spice and the essence of the lotus flower. For the final ingredients shalt thou seek out the perfumes of the Sons of Horus, Lords of the Four Quarters. Mix them carefully, and use the scent in thy chambers to further the work of thy Lord."

9. Then did I step out into the sunlight, seeing the return of the Temple priests. Strong are they, of upright bearing, not from pride, but filled with the essence of the Great God. With them do I glorify Him, and seek to further my knowledge of His Will.

4. ISIS

As we have already seen, Isis has a large part to play in the legend of Osiris, and it is only with difficulty that the two have been separated for analysis. Up to the time of the death of Osiris, Isis is fairly unimportant - her main task being the governing of the country while Osiris was travelling abroad.

According to the legend, as soon as Isis heard of the murder of her husband, she cut off a lock of her hair and put on white mourning garments, as is the custom in Egypt. She did this at Koptos, which has been known ever since as the city of mourning, and then wandered the countryside looking for the fabulous chest. She asked everyone she met if they had seen it, but all said they had not. At last she spoke to a group of children at play, who told her that they had seen her brother Set and his henchmen throwing the chest into the sea.

At about the same time, Isis discovered that Nephthys, the wife of Set, had once disguised herself as Isis in order to trick Osiris, whom she loved, into making love to her. Nephthys had conceived a son, but knowing what Set would do to both of them should he find out, she had abandoned the child. Isis tracked the infant using hunting dogs, and then brought him up to become her guard and attendant, naming him Anubis, Guardian of the Gods.

Returning to search for the chest she followed the coastline, asking all the children along the way if they had seen it. Eventually she came to the country of Byblos, where the chest had been washed up into the fronds of a tamarisk bush that rapidly grew up to enclose the chest in its trunk.

Isis

The tree grew so straight and tall that the King of Byblos, amazed at its size, cut it down to make a pillar for his palace. Isis discovered this, and made up her mind to obtain a post in the palace so that she could get near the pillar. She sat by the side of a fountain in the palace grounds, where the Queen's handmaidens came to rest in their leisure time. She refused to speak to any of them, and so finally the chief handmaiden was summoned. Isis massaged her, and taught her to plait her hair - an unknown thing in that country - all the while using her magic to give the woman a wonderful scent, the secret of which is known only to the gods.

This scent was noticed by the Queen, who asked for Isis to be brought to her to find out the secret of the heavenly perfume. Isis refused to tell her, but wishing to keep her close the Queen made the Goddess nurse to one of her sons. Isis nursed the child well, but in a most unusual manner. She gave him her finger to suck instead of her breast, and each night she put him in a special magical fire in order to consume his mortality while she took on the form of a swallow and flew round the pillar mourning her husband.

This went on for some time, until one night the Queen happened upon them and in terror snatched the child from the fire. Isis then revealed herself in her true form, and told the Queen that she had deprived her son of eternal life, for had he spent one more night in the magical fire he would have awakened as an immortal. The King and Queen asked Isis to stay in Byblos and be worshipped, but she refused. She drew the pillar from its place and removed the chest from it. She then wrapped the empty column in fine linen, poured myrrh and other perfumed oils on it, and gave it to the King so that a shrine to Osiris could be built.

Returning to Egypt she retired to a desert place, and removed the body of Osiris from the chest. She used magic taught to her by her uncle, Thoth, to unite with the body of her husband, and conceived a son who she named Horus, who was born on the Winter solstice - the beginning of the coming of the sun. She had a servant bring him up on the island of Buto and hid the chest with the body of Osiris in a remote region of the country.

Isis frequently visited Horus on the island of Buto, and on one occasion that she was away Set, who was hunting wild pigs, chanced upon the chest and tore the body of Osiris into fourteen pieces, dispersing them throughout the country. Isis soon discovered this, and set off once more in search of the pieces. It is said that she made the first boat out of papyrus in order to travel the Nile in her search, and it is for this reason that crocodiles never touch people in papyrus boats, even to this day, thinking that Isis is still searching for Osiris.

Each time Isis found a part of the body, she made a shrine to him, burying a replica of the whole body there and telling the priests that it was the real body in order to confuse Set, should he ever try to destroy the body again. She eventually found all of the parts except the phallus, which was eaten by a fish, but Thoth fashioned a substitute which has come to be revered as the Tet of Osiris.

Anubis embalmed the body of Osiris, making the separate parts into a unified whole, and used his skills to make the body ready for new life. Isis wanted to bring life to the body, but nothing could be given life without the sacred name of Ra, who has made all things. Isis therefore fashioned a cobra out of clay, moulding into it poison and the spittle of Ra, who in his manifested form had grown very old and tended to dribble. She placed it by a path that Ra frequently passed along.

Later, when Ra was walking along the path, he saw the cobra. Admiring the craftsmanship of its maker he gave it life, and it promptly bit him. Because it was not made by his hand, he could not remove the poison, and fell down in agony. He called all the Gods to him, but none could save him until at last Isis came forward. She told Ra that she would save him only if he would tell her his true name, and he agreed. At first he tried to trick her by reciting a long list of his titles, but she caused the poison to intensify in effect and at last he gave in and whispered his true name to her, giving her permission to pass it on to Horus. For this reason she is known as the Mistress of Magic.

With the power she needed, Isis returned to the embalmed body of Osiris and breathed life into it. Osiris was established as the King of the Underworld, and Isis then turned her mind to preparing Horus for battle with Set, and for his eventual triumph and rule of Egypt.

Isis, known to her priests as Aset, was renowned as the Mistress of Magic. As the wife of Osiris she had political power too, and as She Who Knows the Name of Ra she was considered powerful among the Gods, and is still regarded so today. In the legend we see many instances of her great wisdom and courage, not to mention magical feats. Both Thoth and Khonsu (the Moon God) taught her everything that they knew of magic, so it is not surprising that she was worshipped both in Egypt and overseas.

Her symbol is the throne, and she is often shown wearing this on her head. This shows her importance in the transmission of kingship - as she fought for and won the throne for Horus, she was said to do the same for each Pharaoh, because all Pharaohs were regarded as incarnations of Horus. Her special amulet, the Tyet or "Knot of Isis", is related to the ankh as a symbol of royal and divine power, and in the Book of the Dead appears to represent the blood of the Goddess.

As I have already said, Isis shares the sphere of Chesed with Osiris. She has many similarities with him, and they may be actually seen as male and female aspects of the same force. The colour of Chesed is blue - the colour of Isis - and Chesed is the sphere of building upon the initial creation. It is no surprise that the sphere from which all Holy Powers emanate houses the supreme practitioner of the magick art.

Because of Isis' selfless devotion, courage and protective attitude towards both Osiris and their son, she is seen as a goddess of protection, especially of children. She was thought to be present at the birth of royal children, and many spells for the protection and healing of their children were used by the Ancient Egyptians.

Isis comes down to 20 in the modern numerological system, and 134 in the old system, reducing to 2 and 8. looking at correspondences, we get quite a few relevant items. The first appearance of Isis in Egyptian scriptures depicts her forecasting the death of her brother Osiris, and so it is no surprise to find as one of her correspondences the zodiac wheel, used for divination throughout the ages. As the goddess of wisdom, the correspondence of her name to wisdom and the illuminating intelligence is of no surprise, nor is devotion, the life force, nor the grave which was her longstanding enemy. As Mistress of Magick her correspondences with the magus, the inner Robe of Glory, and the third eye are not inappropriate, either.

The influence of Mercury can be seen throughout the legend as a series of unexpected events, and her strong links with Anubis are also self evident. In fact, everything corresponding to her name fits in with the legend to add strength to her vibration. The attribution of the narcissus as both her flower and her perfume, and turquoise and opals as her stones can also be considered quite correct, as they fit in with her name. Aset comes to nine in the new system, and thirty-two or five in the old. From this we get a correspondence with the sphere of Mars, giving strength and the vision of power, with energy and the spirit of life. The Sphere of Luna gives her magical strength, and the perfumes of the temple and the sandals worn within the temple are sacred to her.

So we see that the correspondences of her name add weight to her legend. Let us look at the gematria of the numbers we have found, and see what lies there. When we do so, we see purity, unity, love and glory linked with the vision, the will, and fraternity. Isis equates with the Garment of Purity, splendour, and above all equilibrium. Her colour, blue, is the colour associated by spiritualists with healing. In my personal system, it is equated with spirituality and communication. It relates to the element of Air, which embodies these principles, and is found in the eastern quarter, location of the throne of the Magus in Qabalah magick.

While I have said a fair amount on the place of Isis, it is almost impossible to express in words the sheer wonder and sensation of total and unconditional love that one feels when the Isis ray is invoked. All I can say is that you, the reader, must simply meet her. Isis is a truly unforgettable experience.

Numerologically, Isis, as a two, is a being with a strong lunar side, containing hidden secrets and hidden depths, with a definite dark side. Her outer and inner aspects are a perfect balance of power and authority. She has much inner strength, and is very much a lunar archetype. Her two adds to the eight of Osiris to give ten, the number of completion, showing them to be the perfect complement.

The main symbol of Isis is her Knot. Looking a little like a drooping ankh, it is also known as her Buckle, and is said to represent her blood. It conforms to the uterus, vagina, and fallopian tubes of a mature woman, and is seen esoterically as the Great Womb without which we would not be. It was used as a symbol of protection and as an amulet for fertility.

The other symbol special to Isis is the Throne. Her name is written with the hieroglyph of the throne, and it is she, in the person of the Queen of Egypt - also the High Priestess of the Mysteries - who enabled the Pharaoh to occupy the throne of the Land. In this context we see her as the "power behind the throne", supporting and empowering her husband Osiris. Indeed, one interpretation of Asar is "He who occupies the Throne".

The experience of meditating on Isis is never the same twice. She will appear in a form appropriate to your situation at the time. Call her to protect your children, and she will come with wings outstretched to cover them. Call her to heal and she will radiate healing energies. Call her to teach or for ritual celebration of her mysteries and she will reveal her power to you.

Many people make the mistake of seeing her only as a gentle mother-figure, but at heart she is a warrior and represents the powerful forces of generation. Beauty and harmony are her ways, but beneath the softly rounded form of this sweet and gentle lady are muscles of steel and a will of white-hot iron. If you become attracted to the gods of Egypt, you will find yourself loving Isis with all your heart, no matter who you choose to serve from the Company of the Gods, for she is beloved of gods and men.

She will help you with your children, and will protect you and that which is yours. She is an excellent healer, both of mind and body, and can teach you the ways of the magic of nature better than any other deity. It is no accident that her worship in classical times spread throughout the known world, for her beauty and wisdom were known by all. Evidence has been found of temples to her in London and York, and in modern times the Fellowship of Isis sees her image in all the goddesses of the world - ten thousand people in over sixty countries find in Isis a goddess they can identify with, and her archetype is correspondingly one of the most active in this modern world of ours.

PATHWORKING

Each of the chapters on the gods will have a section like this. It is a guided spiritual journey to encounter the deity in a way that will enhance your understanding of him or her. The journeys will have a spiritual effect on you that increases with each one you do. You can either do them in the order that they appear in the book, or follow the order of deities in the correspondence tables in appendix 3.

You will need to prepare yourself for the journey. Ideally, have someone there to read the journey to you, or record it on cassette, and play it back to yourself. Seat yourself in a comfortable chair, and take a few moments to get as comfortable as you can. Try not to cross your legs or arms as this is a defensive posture that will lessen your concentration. After you have taken a few deep breaths, and you feel really comfortable, begin your tape or get your partner to read the journey to you. At the end of the journey, have a good stretch and a hot drink - in Ancient Egypt it was traditional to drink hot chocolate after spiritual work. Now for the journey itself.

You find yourself walking in a garden by the river. The rich black soil of the flowerbeds contrasts with the fine white sand of the paths, and as you walk you become aware that you are wearing a white robe. It is just before dusk, and the air is pleasantly cool after a hot day.

Listening to the sounds of birdsong, you sit down in the shade of a palm tree, watching the Nile flowing past you. The scents and sights relax you, and it is a while before you realise that someone is standing beside you. Looking up, you see a beautiful lady in a pleated robe, and a headdress that looks like a golden bird with wings dropping down either side. Her eyes sparkle as she looks down at you, and she extends her hand to help you rise.

As you touch her hand, you feel power and love, much like that of Osiris, but there is also a quality difficult to describe - a feeling of ageless beauty that takes hold of you and strips you of all imperfections.

Before you realise it, you are on your feet in the warm embrace of the Lady Isis. Secure in her arms, you become aware of the suggestion of wings folded about you, and you realise that you are in the safest place in the universe. Then Isis speaks.

"Now that you have found my embrace, sweet child, no thing shall ever harm you. For though you return to your own realm, though you journey to other, distant realms, my wings of protection shall ever be about you."

She releases you, and walks with you through the garden. Neither of you speak, but you notice that with her near the flowers are more brightly coloured, the water of the Nile sparkles, and the setting sun seems almost to bow in respect to her.

You then realise that you are alone in the garden, and even that fades, as you return to your own physical self, and the journey is ended.

MEDITATION

1. In the beauty of the night sky I behold Thee, O Isis, and my heart is light with Thy Presence. O Thou who art Consort to Thy Brother, the Lord of All, I do bow to Thy beauty, and honour Thee with every act of love.

2. Quietly, as a lark's whisper to the setting Sun, do I hear Thy words in my mind, O Goddess, and my very soul is filled with rapture at Thy touch. Be Thou the Governess of my emotions, that I may love and serve Thee and Thy Husband, Osiris of the One Face, with the purity of perfect Truth.

3. Within the rays of the Silver Disk do I see the form of the Goddess, and the words of Her mouth fill me with the purest passion of worship. Thus saith the Queen of Magick: "My heart is warmed, and My words spring forth at thy call, O Prophet. The servant of My Lord shall receive in full that which I do hold secret, and great shall be his attainment.

4. With Truth at My side do I say unto thee, that the strength of My Secret Words are with thee, though thou knowest them not. My powers I give unto thee in the form of Pure Love, that thou mayest pass unto thy followers the beauty of the ancient peace that all lands do crave. Be thou now attendant upon My words, for in them is a secret greater than thou will at first perceive. Unto thee I give the Word of this time, and that Word is Maat, the perfect Truth that knows no restraints.

5. Be thou mindful of this Word, for the end of its path is one of True Knowledge, and the Name of that Knowledge is JERUMAEM, which is a word worthy of study and interpretation; for just as Khepera transforms itself, so shall this Word grow and flower like the lotus stem into a thing of beauty and purity.

6. Learn thou the hidden meaning of this Word, which thou shalt do with the strength of MAAT beside thee, and then truly will thou be like unto a God."

5. HORUS

Horus is the falcon-headed "Lord of the Sky". In one of the texts he is called "Horus the child with his finger in his mouth", because of his birth and secret rearing by Isis. The place of his birth was Khemmis, in the northeast Nile Delta, and he was traditionally hidden on the island of Buto, which eventually merged with the bank of the Nile in the papyrus marshes - hence his title "Horus who is upon his papyrus plants". As a child, he was known as Har-pa-khered (the true Egyptian name was Har, not Horus), which the Greeks changed to Harpocrates.

Because of his upbringing in the swamps, Horus learnt to co-exist with the crocodiles, snakes, scorpions, lions and antelopes, and his figure was often used as an amulet to ward off attacks by these creatures. He was also trained in the fighting arts by the spirit of his dead father, in preparation for the inevitable day when the child would battle with his father's killer, Set. When at last this time came, they and their followers battled for three days.

During one of their personal battles, Set destroyed Horus' eye, which Isis restored with spittle from Ra. The restored eye became his symbol, the Udjat Eye, or Eye of Horus. This is a human eye within cosmetic and falcon cheek markings, and it became the supreme symbol of protection, placed in mummy wrappings and worn on necklaces. To the Ancient Egyptians it stood for the strength of the monarch, protection against Set, and purification.

Finally, the chaotic Set was taken prisoner - but this was only the beginning of the battle. There then began a lengthy

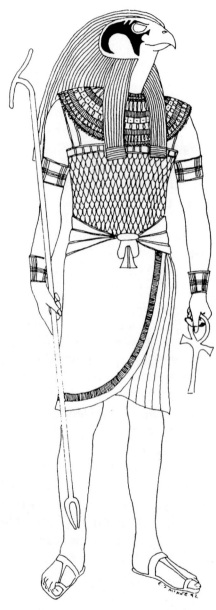

Horus

court of the Gods, in which Set's accusation of Horus' illegitimacy was finally refuted with the aid of Thoth. During this legal action many tricks were played by both sides.

During the course of the hearing, the sympathy of the Gods was obviously with Isis, and Set finally refused to continue if she was present. The tribunal adjourned to an island in the Nile, and the only ferryman was ordered to refuse passage to Isis. Knowing of this, she disguised herself as her sister, Nephthys, who was separated from Set, and was carried across. Enticing Set away from the court, she told him of a youth whose inheritance of his dead father's cattle had been stolen by a stranger. Set expressed anger at this, saying that the youth should have what was his. Isis, still pretending to be Nephthys, told him that she would be by his side once more if he promised her before the court that her son would inherit all that had been his father's. This he did, and at that point Isis removed her disguise and the court forced Set to keep his word - to give Horus the rule of Egypt. Horus was then named Yun-Mutef ("Pillar of his Mother") in commemoration of his success. He was also called Har-nedjitef ("Horus the Saviour of his Father"), for the same reason.

In a cosmic sense, Horus became equated with Ra as the Sun God, depicted as a falcon whose wings were the sky, whose right eye was the sun, and left eye the moon. This was used to further establish the right of a pharaoh to rule, as he was supposed to be the manifestation of Ra, Egypt's first pharaoh, as well as being the son of Osiris and Isis. As the concept of divine kingship developed, Horus came to represent the pharaoh, and the successful legal action brought by Horus to prove his right to rule was seen as being re-enacted by each new pharaoh, to win approval by the Gods.

There are many regional variations of Horus, but as they are mostly "Horus of..." and have much the same appearance, they may be considered to be relevant to particular shrines rather than to the God himself. One exception is Horus of Edfu. The nome of which Edfu was the capital was known as the Throne of Horus, and was apparently the site of the largest battle between Set and Horus. It was here that they transformed themselves into various animals, and it was here that Set was eventually taken captive. Even though as a sun god his main temple was at the Royal Palace, Edfu became the centre of an order known as the Followers of Horus.

The ideas of the Followers of Horus were similar to and pre-dated those of the priesthood of Aten (the solar disk), who attained prominence under Pharaoh Akhnaten, the monarch traditionally accredited with founding the Order of the Rose Cross. It may be that the priesthood of Aten evolved from the F.O.H., or that at some point the two joined forces - what is sure is that orders deriving from both sources have a great deal in common, the main difference being that while the Rose Cross has a decidedly European flavour, the descendants of the Followers of Horus tend to retain a simplicity and Egyptian flavour in their rituals.

Horus gradually assumed the mantle of an older form of himself, Horus the Elder, and indeed some organisations refer to Ra and the two Horus' as all being incarnations of the Solar Logos (principal of the Sun) on different planes. As a falcon, Horus represents the ability to travel between the planes, and his legend depicts overcoming great odds to attain one's goal.

As we have seen, Tiphareth, the sphere that houses Horus, is at the centre of a hexagram of spheres. This is not immediately evident in the traditional representation of the

Tree of Life because the sphere of Daath, situated on the path between Binah and Chokmah, is not usually shown. Daath (the Abyss) is itself at the centre of a hexagram, and represents the division between that which is God and that which comes from God.

The sphere of Tiphareth is the Sphere of the Sun, and is the life-giver and source of being, the ultimate symbol of manifesting energy. Tiphareth is the central pivot of the Tree of Life, being in the centre of the Middle Pillar. The six spheres around it represent the archetypal man, and the central sphere may be considered to be a link between physical incarnation and the upper spheres. It is the highest point of the Tree that ordinary religion reaches - for example, Christ as a sacrificed god is found here, the Station of the Crucifixion. In Tiphareth, God is made manifest. In other words, this is the point at which God becomes understandable to the human mind at its normal level. This sphere is regarded as the Son, Kether being the Father, and all of this reinforces the idea of Horus being the manifestation of Ra, who is himself a manifestation of Atum. In this way all things can be seen to reflect their creator, whether that creator is called the Void, God, Atum, or any one of countless names.

In Qabalistic tradition, the Child-God grows up to become the Saviour who returns equilibrium to the Universe. But this sphere is also the home of the Illuminating God, not only as the Sun God who lights up the world, but more importantly as the god who lights up the consciousness, the soul. In order to transcend this point on the Tree, a magician must take into himself this illumination. To do this he must let go of himself as a man, and be reborn into the sphere of Kether-Atum, forsaking the reflection for the true light. This does not mean that the reflection, that which we normally call reality, is of no value - far from it! Without the reflection the magician would never have reached this far, but like all magical tools and beliefs there comes a point when what was a crutch becomes a limitation, and this is the point to let go of it.

From this we see that Horus may be considered to be the manifestation of the First Initiator, the Holy Guardian Angel. In some systems this being is first encountered in the form of Horus, or as a bird/falcon.

Numerically, Horus gives twenty-seven reducing to nine in the new system, and 208 reducing to ten in the old. These numbers give correspondences of the temple perfume and sandals, the altar, the magic circle and triangle, and the pentagram showing that Isis really did pass on her knowledge to Horus. Other correspondences include works of vengeance (the theme of his legend), the Holy Guardian Angel (showing the truth of his being in Tiphareth) and the Kingdom, showing that he was destined to inherit his father's rule, whatever the odds.

If we take the Egyptian, Har, we get nineteen reducing to ten from the new system, and 107 reducing to seventeen and then eight in the old. This gives us Horus as a warrior, overcoming the evil serpent, attaining the Vision of Splendour with the aid of Thoth, and bringing forth the Children of the Voice (the Sons of Horus). Look at all these correlations, and you will see what Horus represents - the highest point that a human being may reach, the blueprint of perfected mankind.

Numerologically, Horus is a nine, a being of great strength, but one who can lose track of the goal. His main characteristic is strength, and he has great inner strength to go with his physical power. The word "strength" sums him up. He appears as a muscular man with the head of a hawk, wearing a white kilt, the double crown of Egypt, and sometimes the leather tunic of an Egyptian soldier. He can also be seen as a crowned hawk.

His symbol is the Eye of Horus, which is used in the fraction system of Egyptian mathematics: each section represents a fraction; one half, one quarter, one eighth, one sixteenth, through to one sixty-fourth. The sum total of the Eye is 63/64, the final portion being said to be provided by the wisdom of Thoth.

Horus is a warrior, and this certainly shows when his archetype is contacted. He will not accept any beating around the bush, but acts directly, efficiently and promptly, provided your request is just. He is best used for protection of people or property, although he does have a healing aspect.

The strongest impression of Horus is that he is the type of leader who leads from the front. In a war movie he would be John Wayne, letting his actions speak for him as he leads his men by example. One word of warning: Horus is a concrete thinker, so be careful what you say to him - he can be a bit literal.

PATHWORKING

Each of the chapters on the gods will have a section like this. It is a guided spiritual journey to encounter the deity in a way that will enhance your understanding of him or her. The journeys will have a spiritual effect on you that increases with each one you do. You can either do them in the order that they appear in the book, or follow the order of deities in the correspondence tables in appendix 3.

You will need to prepare yourself for the journey. Ideally, have someone there to read the journey to you, or record it on cassette, and play it back to yourself. Seat yourself in a comfortable chair, and take a few moments to get as comfortable as you can. Try not to cross your legs or arms as this is a defensive posture that will lessen your concentration.

After you have taken a few deep breaths, and you feel really comfortable, begin your tape or get your partner to read the journey to you. At the end of the journey, have a good stretch and a hot drink - in Ancient Egypt it was traditional to drink hot chocolate after spiritual work. Now for the journey itself.

You are walking over sand, and you see ahead of you a soldiers' camp. As you get closer, you can see soldiers practicing with their swords, and a few officers practicing manoeuvres in their chariots. One chariot is stationary, and you walk towards it. The charioteer is dressed finely in a white kilt and tunic with golden armour. His helmet appears to be fashioned like a hawk's head, and a red cloak hangs from his golden collar. He beckons you to enter the chariot, and no sooner are you in than he sets the horses galloping across the sand. The sensation is exhilarating, as he skillfully controls the horses with body movements, the reins being tied around his waist. You turn to comment on his skill, and look into the bright eyes of Horus.

The hawkshead is no longer a helmet, but part of the warrior before you. His body is tanned and muscular, and the thrill of the ride is made greater by the knowledge that Horus is champion of all warrior skills. No words are said as you speed across the sand, but you are aware of the fact that as Horus controls the potential chaos of the chariot and horses, he brings order to the chaos of our lives.

Horus senses that his point has been made, and the chariot slows to a halt, back where it started at the camp. You are about to thank Horus when you realise that once again you are with the young mortal officer that you set off with, so you thank him for the demonstration, and walk away. Once again, all fades as the journey draws to an end.

MEDITATION

1. Wondrous is Thy glory, O dawning Son of the Sun, Thou Horus of the Two Horizons. Many are Thy servants, and pure is Thy strength in the sight of the Great God, Thy Father. Thy Mother doth comfort Thee, and Thy servants prepare great feasts in Thy name, O Lord of the Battleground and of the Court.

2. Be Thou with me, Golden Hawk, and let Thy strength descend upon the servant of Thy Father. I see Thy glorious radiance, and hear the Words of Thy Mouth striding forth to place themselves in purity at the seat of my very soul.

3. Thy words are such: "Throughout the times of many men have I searched for the honour that doth come unto the Greatest of Gods, and in Truth do I say that even as the strength of a man fades with his ageing, so doth the memory of his deeds with the ageing of mankind. Seek not for the vain glories of men's achievements, but strive to be perfect in all matters pertaining to the Great God - that is the greater honour, to say that thou hast served the Gods in the course of the Great Work, and hath progressed even unto the utmost that man can attain to. Do thou this in My Name and in that of My Father, the God of One Face, and truly shall thy name ring out in the Hall of

the Double Maati, where no name or deed shall ever be lost, nor go unrewarded.

4. But more I must speak unto thee, of great import to thy work upon this earth. Let thou go forth upon the face of the world, and find for thyself the ones who feel in their souls the call of the ancient ways, and teach thou them to love and to worship without fear, and to perform the deeds of the Great Work in Truth and Purity. And that Great Work shall be the creation of a new unity in the world of men, that no man may be in fear of his neighbour, and that all men shall at length attain their ultimate potential in the eyes of the Gods.

5. Teach thou them the ways of the mind, for therein lies many secrets that thou canst use for the ends of the Great Work set forth for thee. And this also do I say unto thee, that for every man is there a Great Work to be done, and for thee is the task of divining that task, that thou mayest the better enable them to achieve it, thereby achieving thine own sacred task.

6. And when thou hast attained the highest pinnacle, must thou find a successor to continue the Work, as must all who work with thee when they reach this summit, for then shall thou be received into the Halls of thy Lord, My Father, Osiris un-Nefer. At this the world doth fall around me, and the very Gods appear in vast form and glorious arrays of colour and luminance. And the voice of the Nameless Supreme Being doth call forth in words of indescribable beauty, such words that even the Company of Gods, the Lesser Gods and the Greater Gods, do unite in oneness with the whole cosmos, and sight and sound for me are no more, and all is darkness.

6. SET

Set is probably the most maligned deity in the Egyptian pantheon. He was originally a royal deity, held in especially high esteem in the Delta region. However, due to a millenium's worth of bad press, Set is more commonly known as the enemy of Osiris. This attribute only came into being around the time of the Pyramid Texts, and despite occasional royal patronage right up to the Twentieth Dynasty, he was seen as a murderer and champion of Chaos from then on.

In reality this is not completely true, as we shall see: Set represents not true Chaos, but the forces of dispersion necessary to prevent order from becoming stagnant and decadent. Set is the one who presents us with life's charming little challenges, such as divorce, natural disasters and two-year old children.

Much of the legend regarding Set's battle with Horus has been related in the chapters on Osiris, Isis, and Horus. The battle between Horus and Set was vicious, during which Set lost a foreleg and his testicles as they fought in different animal guises. For his crimes, he was condemned to carry Osiris on his shoulders for eternity, but he was not alone in his punishment - his seventy-two fellow conspirators were beheaded.

But this wasn't the end of Set, for he had supporters in high places. Ra supported his claim because he was older than Horus, and even after Set had finally lost the battle for the throne, he remained in Ra's favour. Ra announced that Set was to live with him as his son, to speak out as thunder from the sky. As Lord of the Northern Sky, he was responsible for

Set

storms and clouds, and was often appealed to for good weather for special occasions. He provides an essential service for Ra, too: as the Sun Boat sinks into the western horizon, the serpent Apophis attempts to swallow it, but Set spears the serpent from the bow of the Boat.

Set was rightly thought of as a dangerous and wild deity, but one who protected the throne of Egypt. For the common people, though, his reputation of evil seemed richly deserved, for they believed that he seized the souls of the dead, ate excrement for nourishment, and dwelt in perpetual darkness. Even his name was a source of confusion, being written as Set, Seth, Setekh, Sutekh, Setesh, and Suty. The Greeks identified him with their Lord of Chaos (Typhon, from which we derive our word "typhoon") because of his chaotic nature, and his totem creature is called the Typhonian Beast for this reason.

Set was often portrayed with the head of this creature, which has a curved muzzle and two rectangular ears on top of its head. The Typhonian Beast has no obvious correlation to any creature currently known to science. He was also a notorious shape-changer, appearing in many different forms including a crocodile, a panther, a donkey and snake with the head of an ass. In Ptolemaic rites he was symbolically strangled in the form of a goose.

His colour is red, and the red ox used to be sacrificed in his honour. The pig was sacred to him, so much so that the followers of the cult of Horus considered it to be a taboo animal, and its flesh unhealthy to eat. The hippopotami that occasionally rampaged, overturning boats and trampling crops, were seen as Set's minions, and had to be slaughtered. It was said that Priests at Horus at Edfu ritually ate cakes shaped like hippopotami whilst standing in front of a relief showing Horus destroying Set, to emphasise his impotence.

As has previously been mentioned, Set's colour was red, and he is very occasionally depicted as fully human, with reddish skin and red hair. He was Lord of the Desert, the wasteland and the storm, and ruled over the rotting of corpses that enables their matter to return to the life-cycle. Although Set is a chaotic being, a destructive and negative force, he is nevertheless necessary to balance the positive forces of nature.

Set is a common scapegoat figure in literature. Many stories have him in some guise as a force of evil, and as Typhon he is used in such ways by many forms of magic. He appears as guardian of the tenth Aethyr in Enochian magick, and is considered by many to have been the downfall of Aleister Crowley - having experienced the Set ray, all I can say that if Crowley was as arrogant as his critics have said, then Set would have been attracted to him as a fly to a piece of rotting meat. There is nothing Set likes better than giving the complacent a taste of their real worth.

The colour of Set is that of blood, and in one ancient rite of destruction he is summoned to suck the blood out of the victim. The blood-red of his hair and garb has a much deeper significance. The off-red of congealing blood has a particular significance to those who are able to perceive energies as colours: it is the colour of lust and of sexual energy that is misdirected or out of control. Set is renowned for his foul temper, and the Martian influences of his war-like persona are in keeping with his red hair.

He does however have a more positive side. In his role of Royal Protector, he makes an excellent guardian provided he is handled correctly. He can even be used as an oracle, although great expertise is required to coerce him into total truthfulness.

Using his modern name (Set) in the modern numerical system, we get 152, which adds up to eight. Correspondences for this number give the left hand, the intellect, the Gates of Death, Mars, and the Deceivers. These equate quite nicely with the way he is perceived in modern times.

Taking the Greek form (Typhon) in the old system we get 219, which adds up to 12 or three. Three equates to the Sphere of Saturn, crimson, the Vision of Sorrow, Satan, and the Concealers. Twelve equates to falsehood and dishonesty. Sound familiar? Taking the most common ancient form (Sutekh) in the old system we get 570, adding to twelve or three, which is, of course the same as that of Typhon.

Set's placement in the Sphere of Geburah shows very well the fact that he is not totally evil, but rather a force that is destructive if not carefully balanced and controlled. Numerologically, Set is seen as being concerned with law and order, but his strong mercurial and individualistic streak, coupled with his earthiness and lustfulness, make him liable to rebel against law and order - unless he makes the laws. He is not to be trusted. His influence can be seen in our society even in peacetime, where it manifests as the devouring nature of industry and big business, amongst other things. Only now, as we enter the Age of Horus, are these effects beginning to be redressed in an effort to balance the effects on our planet.

Used properly, Set's power can add resolve to man's endeavours - but his manifold lies and deceits make control very difficult. Worse still, they make it almost impossible to register that there is a problem to start with.

Set's symbol is a composite creature, with a long curved beak, upright square-tipped ears, and cruel eyes. With four legs and a thin weedy tail it looks very strange, but Set takes the head of this creature (known only as the Sethian creature) for his own, being otherwise human in appearance. He wears a kilt, and often carries a staff or knife. There is much speculation on the origin of this creature. Some see it as an example of a now-extinct species, while others see it as a creature from the home of the gods on Sirius. But most scholars agree that its demonic form is a composite of several animals because there was no one creature that summed Set up well enough.

Meditating on Set is a strange experience. When he wants to he can come across as a lovable rogue, but beneath the flannel there is the glint of steel. When working with Set you have to be very careful, because he is the master of deceit and will trip you if he possibly can. It is possible to make use of Set in exercises of spiritual progress, but make sure that you are familiar with the other deities first, because a call to Osiris or Horus is the only thing that will stop him if he gets through your defenses - more than one person has gone mad from unwise contact with Set. The safest thing is to avoid working with him at all, but at some point you must face up to him, and to that part of him that is within us all.

PATHWORKING

Each of the chapters on the gods will have a section like this. It is a guided spiritual journey to encounter the deity in a way that will enhance your understanding of him or her. The journeys will have a spiritual effect on you that increases with each one you do. You can either do them in the order that they appear in the book, or follow the order of deities in the correspondence tables in appendix 3.

You will need to prepare yourself for the journey. Ideally, have someone there to read the journey to you, or record it on cassette, and play it back to yourself. Seat yourself in a comfortable chair, and take a few moments to get as comfortable as you can. Try not to cross your legs or arms as this is a defensive posture that will lessen your concentration.

After you have taken a few deep breaths, and you feel really comfortable, begin your tape or get your partner to read the journey to you. At the end of the journey, have a good stretch and a hot drink - in Ancient Egypt it was traditional to drink hot chocolate after spiritual work. Now for the journey itself.

You are standing on the top of a mountain, just before sunset. The sky is still bright, but the air is cooler. The mountain is to the west of a great valley, and on the far eastern side you can see another mountain just like this one, roughly pyramidal with a flat top.

The sun is low, and seems to be coming towards you. As it gets closer, you recognise the Solar Boat with the sun disk on its bow. The boat pauses for a momentt as it touches the mountaintop, and you climb on board.

No sooner have you boarded the boat than it sinks through the mountain and into the Tuat, the Underworld. Looking forward, you see the back of a muscular figure standing in the bows with a large harpoon. He turns to look at you and you see that he is Set, murderer of Osiris. Then a voice calls you from the centre of the boat.

Ra calls you to him as he stands under the canopy in the middle of the boat. He has the appearance of an elderly man now, and his voice, too, is old as he explains.

"When Set lost the kingdom to Horus, I took pity on him, and he now stands in my boat. It is true that he is an agent of Chaos, and that he has done great wrong. But even the purest evil may serve its purpose in the universe. Watch him, see his task."

Urged forward, you go and stand beside Set, as he watches the waters beneath the bow. "Fear me not, little one," he says, "In this place I can harm you not." Suddenly there is turmoil beneath the boat, and Set strikes out with his harpoon, spearing a massive serpent that is attempting to engulf the boat.

"Look," says Set, "this is the reason I am here. I am filled with hatred and jealousy, but it is my passionate anger that gives me the strength to slay the Apep Serpent. I may be Lord of Desolation, Darkness, and the Desert, but without me there would be no Light."

"When I am freed to do as I will, I cause chaos and destruction, just as the unreigned temper of a mortal can lead him into folly or danger, and cause much harm. But when under the constraints of a Higher Will, that of Ra, I turn my strength and skills to more positive ends. So it is that a mortal under the discipline of the Sacred Mysteries may place his animal passions under the control of his own Higher Will, and cease to be a creature of chaos."

By now, the boat has entered a great chamber, where Ra, now feeble and invalid, is carried to the figure of Osiris standing on the dock. Briefly they merge, becoming one, and when they separate, Ra is young and strong again. He enters the boat and it moves away, rising up until it is atop the mountain to the east of the valley, the dawn of a new day.

You say farewell to Set, and turn to Ra, seeing that he now has a scarab for his head, and thank him for the journey before you step off the boat and watch it rise up into the sky as the sum. Then all fades and you return to your physical realm. The journey is over.

MEDITATION

1. In a night filled with storm do I approach the mountain-top, and stand in my robes of red to meet the Desolate One. Come Thou unto Me, Lord of Those who Howl, and make Thyself known to me. With Maat at my side and the love of my Lord Osiris in my heart do I summon Thee, to speak to me in Truth and Peace.

2. The voice is harsh. Saith the Fiend: "What would I wish to say unto thee, slave of un-Nefer? My words are not for the likes of thee. Summon me when thou hast embraced the void within thy soul, and thou knowest the true desolation of the spirit.

3. I am the Lord of the Vortex of Chaos, the Destroyer who returns all things to the First Form. Putrefaction is my desire, and my sacrifice is one of blood. Fear me mortal, for without thy Lord thou would be sucked into the void by My proximity.

4. But I see that you summon Me not to taunt, nor to command, but to learn of My nature. For that courtesy, frail man, I shall speak in Truth indeed. I am Brother to Thy Lord, and no less exalted, but men fear me for the forces I enfold. Prince of the Sacred Land am I, but My home is in the Wasteland, for I have been cast forth.

5. Show unto Me thy weakness, and I shall destroy thee, but in thy strength I will work with thee towards the Great Work, as do we all. I have claimed men

greater than thee, but none with thy love of My Brother. To love Asar as thou dost, must thou also love Me, for He and I are One and our existence is mutual. For truly, to embrace the void within thy soul is to unite with thyself and pass beyond it.

6. For so great is man's fear of me that he avoids that which I offer. To serve me is to allow the void to embrace thee, but by thy love thou canst embrace the Wasteland and make it whole. Thus do men become Gods, and at this do the Gods rejoice. But listen not to My words, for I am the Deceiving One, and a word from Me to thee is of no worth."

7. The wind doth pull at my robe as I stand before Him. My faith in my Lord Osiris doth make me calm, but I know not of the Truth of the Words of Set. The wind doth die, and He is gone. I remain, alone with my doubts, my fears, and all that maketh me human.

7. NEPHTHYS

Nephthys is a funerary goddess, although to a large extent her legends have been swallowed by her subordinate role in the legends of Osiris. She was the wife and sister of Set, but could bear no children by him. She did give birth to a son, Anubis, but he was fathered by Osiris rather than Set.

There are many signs that her role was originally much greater than that shown by the familiar legend. She is often depicted as suckling the Pharaoh, who is referred to as her "menstrual blood". The wrappings of the mummy were known as the "tresses of Nephthys", and her main role seems to be Goddess of the processes of dispersion, complementing her sister Isis, who presides over the processes of formation. Plays on her name give us words for "weaver" and "tresses", and Nephthys together with her sister Isis are frequently referred to in magical texts as "the two Weavers" or "the Lips of Atum". Many scholars identify Nephthys as the shadow, or dark side, of Isis. Together, they were considered responsible for making the light of creation circulate.

The name of Nephthys (Neb-Hut) also signifies "Ruler of the Temple", and she is most often evoked as a protector from negative forces: since she rules the dispersion process, she also rules the forces that bring about destruction, and cn prevent them from acting on those under her care. Isis and Nephthys were represented by the two plumes on the Sacred Crown, from whence they protected the Pharaoh.

Nephthys is popularly seen a a hand-maiden of Isis, to whom she turned after leaving Set, and as guardian of hidden or concealed things she governs the powers of invisibility and

Nephthys

anonymity. Unfortunately, she is so good at concealing herself from mundane eyes, that there is very little physical evidence on which to base a picture of her. Her only strong image to survive to the modern day is the depiction of Nephthys and Isis as twin cobras on the headband of the Pharaoh.

Nephthys, as a guardian of hidden things, is naturally responsible for revealing such things at the right time, and as so governs the process of psychic receptivity. Her union with Osiris (who represents light, truth, and order) brought about Anubis, the Guide who leads the initiate through the darkness of the afterlife, or the deep realms of the self. Nephthys is often shown wearing a dress of her colour, pale green. Her symbol is the basket (another play on her name), a receptacle for the energies of life which she uses to disperse and reform into new life-force. As a Geburic being her work is often seen as negative, but is necessary in order for her sister Isis to have the materials for her part of the cycle, re-formation.

Let us now look at her name. Nephthys in the new system gives us 35, adding to 8, which shows her as the perfect balance for Set and also a complement for Osiris. Her original name, Neb-Hut, gives 67, adding to 13 and four. Thirteen gives us the Moon, the High Priestess, clairvoyance and menstrual blood, all of which have relevance to the way in which she is perceived. Four gives us mercy, the meaning of Chesed (the Sphere of Osiris and Isis), which indicates that her higher purpose is affiliated to the formation process. Four also gives us the Vision of Love, an attribute the Greeks recognised when they identified her with Aphrodite.

Her numerological analysis is interesting. It shows her as a generous person, giving of herself, very much a stickler for rules - but nonetheless, someone who lives life to the hilt.

Although her primary function is one if dispersion, she has great communicative skills, and has a lot of love to give. Nephthys is pictured as a beautiful lady in a long dress, with a strong resemblance to Isis, and wearing a stylised basket on her head. Her symbol is the basket that she wears, and the two plumes of the Atef Crown represent her and Isis as protectors of the crown's wearer. She is very much like Isis, though she never displays the strength of character that her sister can show when the need arises. Always gentle, always calm, she will tell you what she thinks you should know, and no more. Secrets are her domain, and she will often confuse you because of this. Despite this she is a joy to work with and her power, though gentle, has a lot of force behind it.

PATHWORKING

Each of the chapters on the gods will have a section like this. It is a guided spiritual journey to encounter the deity in a way that will enhance your understanding of him or her. The journeys will have a spiritual effect on you that increases with each one you do. You can either do them in the order that they appear in the book, or follow the order of deities in the correspondence tables in appendix 3.

You will need to prepare yourself for the journey. Ideally, have someone there to read the journey to you, or record it on cassette, and play it back to yourself. Seat yourself in a comfortable chair, and take a few moments to get as comfortable as you can. Try not to cross your legs or arms as this is a defensive posture that will lessen your concentration.

After you have taken a few deep breaths, and you feel really comfortable, begin your tape or get your partner to read the journey to you. At the end of the journey, have a good stretch and a hot drink - in Ancient Egypt it was traditional to drink hot chocolate after spiritual work. Now for the journey itself.

You find yourself once more in the garden by the Nile. You walk for a while, enjoying the sights and scents of the flowers. You notice, however, that the garden is different: although still beautiful, the flowers are beginning to fade and die, coming to the end of their lives. But among the fallen petals on the ground, you can already see the tiny shoots of new plants as the cycle of life continues.

A few yards away you see a figure of a woman. At first, as you walk towards her, you think it is Isis, but this woman is subtly different, as if Isis were a little older, and a little tired. On her head she wears a basket-shaped headdress, and you realise it is Nephthys, the sister of Isis.

"Not merely her sister," says Nephthys, reading your thoughts, "but rather her other self, the dark Isis. As she aids the passage of souls into the physical existence, so do I assist them to leave the world of men, dispersing the matter of their bodies to the elements."

As with Isis, you walk with Nephthys silently through the garden, but you are aware that she can read your every thought, knows all of your secrets. It occurs to you that Isis can do this too, but her liveliness masks the feeling it provokes. Nephthys, more quiet, more melancholy, does not conceal what she does.

"You are right, my child," she says, "Though I have many secrets I do not make a secret of my work. Man tries to keep me from my task, embalming and anointing the dead to make their bodies last forever, but in the end I fulfil my duty, for time is nothing to me. Man fears me, but my power is needed to ensure that man continues to return to the world;

if I did not recycle the matter and energy of all that exists, the universe would soon be devoid of any to make new things, and all would cease."

You turn to her, ready to agree with her, but she places a finger to your lips; she already knows, and your acceptance has revitalised her, for she shines with a radiance beautiful to behold, and between her and her sister Isis no mortal could differentiate.

"You give me a truly great gift, mortal," she says, "let me give you a gift in return, that until your time comes, no forces of dispersion may harm you." With that she is gone, and the garden fades as the light at sunset, and your journey is over.

MEDITATION

1. Dark Mistress of the Temple, I come to you. Embrace me in Thy protecting wings, and let me feel the Truth of Thy Being. Come Thou to me, that I may dissolve in Thy form, and be made anew.

2. The lake is still, and the night is silent, yet I feel Her presence in the waters. "Purification of the Soul" is the name of the lake, and I must enter, for She is within. Cool and green are the waters, and soothing unto my heart, as I see Her in Her Temple of the Heart.

3. She saith: "Greetings, young traveller from the World of Men. Seldom am I visited by those thou callest mortals, for My Mysteries are too dark for the likes of them. But thou, thou seemest different, for thou hast no fear of the processes of dispersion that I

command. Thou biddest me to make thee anew, and thus shall I do, for such as thee are precious to Me.

4. Thou feelest the confusion that doth surround me. Fear it not, for it is but the web that man doth weave, and My web is of a different thread. Come thou to Me, embrace Me, that we may be One."

5. In unity do I behold the beauty of the Dark One, for she Truly is the Sister of Her Mistress, Isis. Caught in a wave of sensual wonder, I lose all sense of that which I term "myself", as the Lady of the Basket doth show unto me the wonders of continuing creation. Rapture fills my soul, and an ecstacy that defies all words, and all too soon doth she return me to the shore of the Sacred Lake.

6. "Not for thee the eternal Void," She saith, "but rather that thou walkest the path of thy predecessors, as a Prophet and Priest. Serve thy Lord, as do I, and take My blessing, that the Lord of Chaos may plant no more doubts in thy heart."

Anubis

8. ANUBIS

The image of Anubis, the god of embalming and guide of the underworld, is possibly the most instantly recognisable of all god-images. The image is a strong one: a well-built man with the head of a black dog, wearing the leather tunic and kilt of a soldier, with a golden collar representing his magical power and mastery of the astral realms. He is often seen in a gateway, or as wholly canine above a gateway. His role in the legends is equally potent, for he is seen as the walker-between-worlds, the guide and protector of Isis as she searched for the body of her lost Osiris.

In funeral texts, Anubis is called "he who counts the hearts", and is seen beside the scales, weighing the heart of the deceased against the Feather of Truth while the impartial Thoth records the outcome. Those who pass the test, he would then guide to the throne of Osiris: those who failed would have their heart fed to an entity known as The Devourer, and without it were damned to the Egyptian version of hell. In the Pyramid Texts, as 'Claimer of Hearts' Anubis frees the Pharaoh from the restrictions of earthly life so that he can take his place among the gods.

Like many gods, Anubis has a bewildering array of titles, examination of which allows a degree of insight into his nature.

KHENTY-AMENTI. "Foremost among Westerners". This refers to his rule of the cemeteries and places of embalming, all situated on the west bank of the Nile.

KHENTY-SEH-NETER. "Presider over the God's pavilion". The pavilion refers both to the embalmer's tent and to the burial chamber itself. This title is a direct reference to the House of Purification (as the embalmer's tent was known) that Anubis built with the help of Thoth for the preparation of the body of Osiris.

Most of his titles refer to his well-known role in the funeral process, but as guide for the souls of the dead, and as herald of the Gods, he was also thought of as a guardian against astral forces. There are many spells for divination in the magical texts that involve scrying in a bowl with the aid of Anubis, who escorts the relevant deity to the vision of the seer. Since Anubis helped Isis in her search for the body of Osiris, he was often called upon for aid when a physical object had been lost. He was also invoked before surgery to protect the unconscious patient whilst away from his physical body and lead him safely back to the physical realm.

In modern magic, Anubis is regarded as the Guardian of the Gateway, the Walker Between Worlds. Situated in the Sphere of Malkuth, he is the Dweller on the Threshold who challenges our right to enter the magickal Universe, and guides us safely to our destination - provided we pass the test. He therefore has an important role in initiation, and many who undergo initiation into the Egyptian Mysteries feel his presence very strongly, both in their lives and in the rite itself.

The name of Anubis comes to 21 in the new numerical system, further reducing to 3. This number equates with Mercury, and his role as herald is thus confirmed. His is the outer robe of concealment, just as the Black Anubis who guards the gate against unworthy supplicants becomes the Golden Anubis who helps us find our goal. In the old system (for which we use Anpu, the original name), we get 131 reducing to 5, the number of the physical realm. It equates to death, judgement of the dead, and the Garden of Mansions (a name for the dwelling place of those among the dead who have successfully undergone the Weighing of the Heart).

Using the Hellenised form, Anubis, we get 123 reducing to 6. This gives the colour gold and the phoenix (symbol of regeneration), devotion to the Great Work, and intuition. From this we can see that the Golden Anubis who regenerates us by the initiatory process, speaks to us through our intuition. His words enable us to continue to exercise our true will and - eventually - to complete the Great Work and thus unite with Atum.

Anubis is the mediator between Osiris and the magician. As Plutach said:

"By Anubis they (the initiates) understand the horizontal circle, which divides the invisible part of the world, which they call Nephthys, from the visible, to which they give the name of Isis; and as this circle equally touches upon the confines of both light and darkness, it may be looked upon as common to them both - and from the circumstance arose that resemblance, which they imagine between Anubis and the dog, it being observed of this animal, that he is equally watchful... by day as [by] night."

So it can be seen that Anubis is in the ideal position to perform his task of assisting man's evolution on both a racial and on a personal level. By ruling over the processes of death and the symbolic death of initiation, and by acting as mediator and oracle, he gently guides those who wish to follow him along the uneven path of spiritual evolution. Numerologically speaking, Anubis as a three is a good communicator, although he can be unpredictable. He is mild mannered, and is slow to give us his love and respect - but once gained it is not easily shaken. He has an enormous amount of love to give, but it is his nature to hide it behind a front of dogmatism (sorry) and efficiency.

Anubis does not waste words. When you encounter him, he speaks directly to you with images and impressions, avoiding the ambiguity of language. Quiet and reserved, he is helpful, courteous and will never permit himself to become angry. He will guide you along the path, and teach you well. Moreover, he has something of the night hunter in his nature, and is a good friend in times of crisis.

PATHWORKING

Each of the chapters on the gods will have a section like this. It is a guided spiritual journey to encounter the deity in a way that will enhance your understanding of him or her. The journeys will have a spiritual effect on you that increases with each one you do. You can either do them in the order that they appear in the book, or follow the order of deities in the correspondence tables in appendix 3.

You will need to prepare yourself for the journey. Ideally, have someone there to read the journey to you, or record it on cassette, and play it back to yourself. Seat yourself in a comfortable chair, and take a few moments to get as comfortable as you can. Try not to cross your legs or arms as this is a defensive posture that will lessen your concentration.

After you have taken a few deep breaths, and you feel really comfortable, begin your tape or get your partner to read the journey to you. At the end of the journey, have a good stretch and a hot drink - in Ancient Egypt it was traditional to drink hot chocolate after spiritual work. Now for the journey itself.

You find yourself outside a walled village on the west bank of the Nile. This is the Necropolis, the City of the Dead. In the cliff above you can see the workmen digging out a tomb in the rock, and craftsmen go about the village doing their jobs cheerfully and efficiently. As you walk through the village, you see a large tent in the centre, and walk towards it. The tent is square, made of silk, and those entering and leaving it wear the robes and regalia of the priesthood.

You step inside the tent, and the first thing you see is a bier on which lies a mummy. The wrappings have obviously just been placed on the mummy, for they are clean, and you can smell the oils and herbs they have been impregnated with.

As scribes lay strips of linen with chapters of the book of the dead upon the body, a priest wearing an Anubis mask intones the words from a papyrus scroll. You listen to the words which, though meaningless to you, have a power and majesty about them. So entranced by the words are you that you do not notice that everyone has left but you and the priest. The voice stops, and you look towards the priest to see not the mask, but the living form of Anubis.

There is a twinkle in his eye, as he gestures to the body, and you become aware that the physical shell contains other bodies, which rise from it one by one, forms of light and energy. Five bodies now stand before you briefly, then you are aware that only the spirit of the deceased remains - the other bodies have gone to their rightful places.

Anubis takes you by the arm, and also he takes the spirit, or ka, by the arm, and the three of you rise up into the air. You travel through mist until you reach a gateway. Anubis stops, beckoning you to remain at the gateway, before guiding the soul through the portal into a chamber beyond.

The doors remain open, and you watch as the spirit is brought to a giant set of scales, and his heart is weighed by Thoth and Anubis before he is led by Horus through another set of doors. Anubis returns to you, takes your hand, and leads you to a river.

Standing on the bank of the river is a man in priestly robes, waiting to cross to the other side, where there is a large temple made from light. He calls out a word, and a boat begins to form in front of him. The ferryman questions him and he answers, then he, you, and Anubis enter the boat.

Anubis stands in the bows, obviously acting as navigator as the boat crosses the river, avoiding sandbanks and dangerous currents. At the other side the priest gets out, thanking Anubis and the ferryman. Anubis takes your arm, and you return with him to the tent and the mummy.

You then realise that Anubis has, without saying a word, explained that he is the guide of both the living and the dead, and you understand that if you choose to walk the path of the Mysteries, he will guide your feet. Anubis smiles, and all fades as the journey ends.

MEDITATION

1. I enter the House of Purification, and all is silent. Come unto me, Lord of the Cemetery, First Embalmer, and let me know Thy ways. Speak Thou unto me of Thy journey through the Tuat, and of Thy wanderings in the desert.

2. He is here, and yet I hear Him not. Silently doth He stand before me, and His eyes are locked on mine. Then, still without a sound, He doth take mine hand, and leadeth me from the tent of the embalmers.

3. Dark is the night, but the Tuat is darker, for He taketh me through the Gate, and we proceed along the Path of Man toward the Underworld.

4. Words come not from He who guards the Goddess, and the words of my mind come slowly, and they are hard to form. The realm unto which He doth take me is like unto nothing that I have formerly seen, and my very self is falling into its separate components.

5. At every Gate that we do pass, I do leave a portion of myself behind, and now do I find that there is nothing to leave, and yet I am still here. Anubis, Jackal-son of Isis, is of golden face, and now do I perceive his words. They are such:

6. "Were I not here, gentle Prophet, thy very being would cease to be. This is my realm, between the worlds, and none may pass through save they pass with My leadership. Thou smellest the scent of My Temples, and thou hearest My voice. Harken to my guidance in thy heart, for thou art precious unto Me.

7. Walk thou for eternity in the ways of Thy Master, for thine is the sacred task. As I am in this world, so thou must be in thine." There is no more, for He leadeth me back upon the way that we have traversed, and with my mind in darkness, do I return to mine own land.

Hathor

9. HATHOR

Hathor was a cow-goddess with a great number of followers. She was seen as the principle of all mothers of pharaohs, just as Horus was to the pharaohs themselves. Her name means "Mansion of Horus", but actually implies "Lady of the Sky", as she is depicted as protecting Horus in her womb. She is the daughter of Ra, and wife of Horus. The Pharaohs were often depicted with Hathor standing by their side, and she, like Nephthys, was said to suckle the king. This indicates her funerary aspect, where she represented the nurturing and continuation of life beyond death.

However, perhaps her most important - and most popular - aspect was her role as goddess of love, music, and dance. She is the supreme goddess of sexual love in Egypt, representing both the turmoil and the ecstacy of physical desire. She has the ability to encourage sensual joy through dance and music. Music was an important part of her rites, too: one of her symbols is the systrum, a sacred bronze rattle which was often made in her image. Her priestess carried sistrums (musical rattles in the shape of the ankh) and musical necklaces called Menats, which were shaken rather than worn. The beautiful Hathor was said to have cured Ra of a sulking fit during the battles of Horus and Set by dancing naked before him until he burst into joyous laughter. The people of insular Khem saw her as the goddess of foreign countries and of Byblos and Nubia in particular, where she was also worshipped. Another area that came under her jurisdiction was the Sinai Peninsula, where the fabulous turquoise mines gave her the title of "Lady of Turquoise".

Do not fall into the trap of seeing Hathor as a "soft" goddess, essence of all the nice things about the female psyche: like all females she had a dark side. Before Egyptian culture refined her into the comfortable, tame figure she is now, Hathor was known as the destructive goddess Sekhmet, the Eye of Ra. Although the two goddesses are linked, they are fundamentally different in aspect and feel, so Sekhmet has been given her own chapter - you will see why when you read it.

In many ways, Hathor is a form of Nut, as she too represents "fertile space", the concept of a vessel that although empty has the potential to generate life. She was also said to preside over all aspects of women's beauty, and in this aspect she acquired the mirror as a symbol, which was both a tool to aid beauty and a potent magical weapon. In this role she was known as the Lady of Sycamore - a tree sacred to her, and one used to provide ash for make-up colouring.

She also has a cosmic aspect, and her role as a Star Goddess is most evident in the persona of Sekhmet, as which she was said to be older than the universe itself... but do not let this distract you from looking at Hathor in her own right, for as the beautiful Hathor she was very much a patron of women. She used her abilities to protect and help them in many ways, and at certain times in Egyptian history she was considered to be a female version of Ra, no less.

She resides in the Sphere of Netzach, where she is seen as a beautiful naked woman. Her Netzachian traits are well displayed in her alter-ego of Sekhmet: in the legends, Ra was angered by conspiracies against him after Isis made a fool of him and sent Sekhmet to earth to punish mankind. There followed such a bloodbath that Ra became fearful that his entire creation would be destroyed and finally ordered her to stop. By this time, though, she was so carried away with blood-lust that she did not hear him. Ra and Thoth arranged for several large vats of beer which had been coloured red with ochre to be placed in her path. Mistaking them for blood, she drank them and fell into a stupor: and then by his magic Ra transformed her while she slept into Hathor, the gentle Goddess of Music and Love.

This legend shows how the apparently gentle emotions of love and enjoyment can get out of control - as in an addiction or obsession - and their surprising strength when this happens. The Sekhmet of this story is the hidden aspect of Hathor that must be acknowledged and accepted in order to work with her.

Hathor comes to 1 in the old numerical system and 7 in the new. One gives us hidden intelligence, concealed light, and death. Seven gives venus, victory, occult intelligence, Hathor, aphrodite, and the vision of Beauty Triumphant. All of these give a clue to her nature. Numerologically, as a seven, she is a generous goddess, though like Nephthys she has an underlying regard for justice. It is her nature to give selflessly, but beneath her benign and nurturing vision lies a passionate being of great strength and power. Forgetting this is a mistake.

Hathor sometimes appears as a cow-headed woman. Her eyes are large and filled with love, and the overall impression is that of the true essence of motherhood. More usually she presents herself as a beautiful woman wearing a headdress of cow's horns and the solar disk. She usually carries a sistrum to symbolise her role as the goddess of music and love, and wears a figure-hugging dress of light coral-coloured fabric - but however she appears, she will always be full of radiant and all-encompassing love.

To experience this archetype is to experience love itself. This most gentle of goddesses can fill you with such joy and music that it often becomes impossible to concentrate on the task in hand, but she is a teacher too. She will teach you to love your fellow humans, and also to love the gods. She will heal, nurture and comfort you, so that you leave her presence rested and refreshed, ready to face your life with enthusiasm.

PATHWORKING

Each of the chapters on the gods will have a section like this. It is a guided spiritual journey to encounter the deity in a way that will enhance your understanding of him or her. The journeys will have a spiritual effect on you that increases with each one you do. You can either do them in the order that they appear in the book, or follow the order of deities in the correspondence tables in appendix 3.

You will need to prepare yourself for the journey. Ideally, have someone there to read the journey to you, or record it on cassette, and play it back to yourself. Seat yourself in a comfortable chair, and take a few moments to get as comfortable as you can. Try not to cross your legs or arms as this is a defensive posture that will lessen your concentration.

After you have taken a few deep breaths, and you feel really comfortable, begin your tape or get your partner to read the journey to you. At the end of the journey, have a good stretch and a hot drink - in Ancient Egypt it was traditional to drink hot chocolate after spiritual work. Now for the journey itself.

You stand outside a temple, in the courtyard. Before you are the steps leading to the entrances, and a row of columns, each capped with the head of Hathor. A sound comes from within the temple, and no sooner have you heard it than a procession of priestesses come dancing into the courtyard, playing sistrums, waving menat rattles, and clinking finger cymbals. As they dance one priestess, standing still, sings a song about love and joy, and although you do not know the words, or the dance, you feel yourself wanting to join in. You listen to the song as it fades away to be replaced by the voice of Hathor.

"Gentle am I, traveller, and my way is the way of happiness. Men call me the Goddess of Love and Music, and my greatest joy is to see the love of one person for another. Gentle is my power, but strong it is, for none may enter the Kingdom of the Justified One unless he loves and is loved."

You realise that the voice is coming from the temple - not from within it, but from the building itself. Hathor tells you that this is because a place that is filled with music and love can become a vessel for her will - and a person filled with music and love will speak the words of the gods.

With the words of Hathor in your heart, you care no longer that no-one has taught you the dance, and you join with the priestesses in a dance that tells of the creation of the world, and of the gods, and of mankind, until all becomes one, the images fade, and the journey is over.

MEDITATION

1. To the sound of the sistrum I call Thy name, O Lady of the Mansion, that I might be filled with the joy of Thee as I watch Thy sacred dance and share Thy music.

2. Come Thou unto me, sweet Spirit of Love, for my heart is sad with mortal fears, and I would be comforted by Thee. Let Thy music and Thy dance uplift me, that I may be sad no more, that I may continue the work which I must do.

3. Fragrant perfume fills my head, as with the rattle of the sistrum she dances before me. Speak to me, Sweet Maiden, for I crave Thy wisdom, and for love of Thee I have no words of my own.

4. "Give thy fears and worries to the creatures of the sea, gentle child, and let the sea purge your heart of its woes. I am here, as I have ever been, and My music is thine. Listen thou to the sounds of thy life; the beating of thy heart is that of My dance, and the cries of joy of thy children are the tunes that I play. Open thy heart unto this wondrous symphony, and there shall be no room for fears, nor room for woes.

5. Love, and be loved. Give that thou mayest receive in full the splendour of life's gifts. Young art thou, yet in many ways art thou ancient, and thine older self cries out for the loss of youth.

6. Come to the Gods like unto a child, and thou will see that all life is to be lived in joyfulness. I am joy, I am love. come unto me, and I shall be thine."

7. With tears in my eye do I thank this gentle Goddess for Her words, and the dance continues, but I remain.

10. SEKHMET

In the earliest of times, long before the appearance of Osiris and his family, Ra reigned peacefully over all of his creation. But as time passed, the manifest god got older, and at last a group of renegades tried to usurp his position and staged a revolt against him. So angered was the sun-god that he plucked an eye from his head, conjured it into the form of Sekhmet, and hurled it at his enemies.

Sekhmet immediately attacked the renegades with vigour, until the land flowed with the blood of her victims. Ra was horrified at the carnage and saw that unless she was stopped she would destroy all of creation. He called out to her, but it was too late - and this story ends as detailed in the previous chapter, with the enforced transformation of Sekhmet into the gentle Hathor.

Another, perhaps more appropriate story states that she heard Ra and stopped her carnage, only to see that he had grown a new eye to replace her. She flew into a melancholy rage and fled into the desert as a wild lion - and so she stayed until at last Thoth was sent to bring her home. He went to her in the form of an agile ape, and using all his skill finally managed to break her mood and taught her that without mercy, severity serves no master but Chaos. He taught her that even the weak can help the strong (using the original version of a tale that, centuries later, Aesop told as the fable of the lion and the mouse). At last he brought Sekhmet home, and Ra received her in joy.

Sekhmet was worshipped at Memphis as the wife of Ptah the Architect God, and with their son Nefertum (later

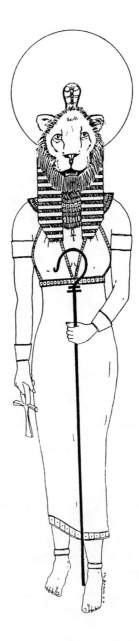

Sekhmet

replaced by Imhotep, god of medicine) they became the divine triad of Memphis. Sekhmet had no temple of her own, but in nearly every royal temple there were statues and reliefs of her. Her followers revered her as a teacher and healer, but she was feared by those who did not follow her path, for obvious reasons. She heals the same way she crushed the revolt - by purging, by "burning out" infection. Likewise, the lessons she teaches are not easy ones, but are necessary none the less.

In modern times, Sekhmet has become a great favourite with students of many pagan ways, as the archetype of all women. To the modern devotee she is the teacher, the mother, the lover, the whore, the guardian, and many other aspects. She represents the wild, untamed side of woman in the same way that the Horned God of the witches represents untamed man. In many ways, Sekhmet is similar to Set, but there is one essential difference: Set personifies the destructive forces of Chaos within Order, while Sekhmet is the Champion of Order.

In the past, much has been made of the link between Sekhmet and Hathor. This link is very real, although both entities exist in their own right, and both have an element of unpredictability that adds a bit of spice to their devotions. Another deity sometimes linked with Sekhmet is Bast, the feline goddess, but the two are really quite different when experienced through ritual or meditation. Of all the deities of Ancient Egypt, Sekhmet is considered to be the oldest. Many texts refer to her as being older than the gods, older than the universe, and other similar terms: she is certainly more fundamental than the Neters (the lesser gods), which are simply the personifications of cosmic attributes. All goddesses can be seen as aspects of Sekhmet, as all gods are aspects of Asar-Ra.

Sekhmet has so many titles that one of them is "Lady of a Thousand Names". Perhaps the most interesting one is "Mistress of Magick", for just as Isis teaches natural magic to initiates, it is Sekhmet who instructs them in the arts of High Magick, the magic that transcends nature, the Star Magick. Her titles reflect her all-encompassing role, and indeed the name Sekhmet simply means "The Powerful".

Being linked closely to Hathor, Sekhmet also occupies the sphere of Netzach, which has many attributions of a magical nature. Like Hathor, she is not afraid to dance naked before us - but her motives are more primal, more basic. Sekhmet is a goddess of great physical passion, and in this area she has her closest links with Hathor. If you owe her a favour, Sekhmet takes her payment in sexual terms - and not in the gently sensual way encouraged by Hathor, either! She is the embodiment of lust in a positive sense, giving forth an incredibly powerful aura of pure life-force.

In both the old and new numerical systems her name comes to 9, the number of power, and of the Triple Goddess of paganism. She is the Pure Intelligence, the embodiment of independence, with great strength. Her negative effect is impotence, so no surprises there, either! Her priesthood were renowned for practicing preventative medicine, which shows her healing style admirably, where the potential of illness is removed by purification of the body. Her priesthood were also famous for their knowledge of the heart, and were even said to have performed open-heart surgery.

For a goddess popularly associated with destruction and yet renowned for her healing qualities, the Ankh is a most appropriate symbol: it is the Key of Life - and of Death. She is aptly considered by modern occultists to be a goddess of both demolition and renewal, making her position as the wife of Ptah the master architect very appropriate.

Numerologically, she is the personification of strength, with a healthy regard for sexual pleasures; but she has a hidden side too, so tread carefully. She finds a feeling of completion through ecstacy, but is a staunch supporter of justice, and will claw as easily as caress if that is what justice demands.

Sekhmet is usually depicted as a lioness-headed woman of beautiful proportions, wearing a tight-fitting long red dress. On her head is the solar disk and the Ureas Serpent that symbolises her wisdom. She usually carries an ankh, and this symbol - although in universal use - is her special tool, for she directs her powerful energies with it, showing that she is Mistress of the Life-Force. Her other symbol is the lion's head, often worn as a pendant or brooch by her devotees.

If you have any old-fashioned or sexist ideas about women, then calling on Sekhmet is likely to be unpleasant for you, for she is all women and all Woman, and demands that you respect her in the form of her sisters, female humans. Accept her and offer her your love, and she will be all things to you, lover, mother, sister, friend, and more.

Mediating Sekhmet has its price. She is the goddess who rules sexual passion, and working with her will increase your sex drive and reduce your inhibitions - my wife and I often joke that a ritual involving her is always followed by a night with very little sleep!

Sekhmet has a reputation for cruelty, but that is due to her task of teaching the unpleasant lessons in life. Just as a mother cat will cuff her kittens away with claws extended as she tries to wean them from her milk, so Sekhmet sometimes has to use her claws to teach us something we have refused to accept. And it is true, if you evoke her anger - by harming or dishonouring a female - she will show no mercy, playing with you as a cat plays with a mouse. When punishment finally comes, it is almost a relief.

So as you can see, she is not a deity to work with lightly, but if she accepts you she will place all of her power behind you, transforming your life in so many ways you will seem to your friends like a different person. Give her your love, for in loving her you love all women - seek the goddess in those around you, and she will be with you forever.

PATHWORKING

Each of the chapters on the gods will have a section like this. It is a guided spiritual journey to encounter the deity in a way that will enhance your understanding of him or her. The journeys will have a spiritual effect on you that increases with each one you do. You can either do them in the order that they appear in the book, or follow the order of deities in the correspondence tables in appendix 3.

You will need to prepare yourself for the journey. Ideally, have someone there to read the journey to you, or record it on cassette, and play it back to yourself. Seat yourself in a comfortable chair, and take a few moments to get as comfortable as you can. Try not to cross your legs or arms as this is a defensive posture that will lessen your concentration.

After you have taken a few deep breaths, and you feel really comfortable, begin your tape or get your partner to read the journey to you. At the end of the journey, have a good stretch and a hot drink - in Ancient Egypt it was traditional to drink hot chocolate after spiritual work. Now for the journey itself.

You find yourself walking through the rocky hills on the west bank of the Nile. Below is the City of Artisans, which houses the artists who paint the scenes in the tombs. The sun is hot, and a breeze blows sand up in your face, making the walk mildly unpleasant, but the view around you is more than compensation for the discomfort.

But the breeze begins to get stronger, and the dusty sand becomes a greater irritant, stinging your eyes and clogging your throat, so you look for shelter. After a few moments, you discover a small opening in the rocks, and enter what you at first perceive as a small cave. It does not take you long to realise, though, that you have entered a natural tunnel into the hillside. The sandstorm outside is getting worse, and a little way into the tunnel you find a reed torch, and with it to light your way, you decide to explore the tunnel until the sandstorm dies away. The tunnel runs straight into the hillside for a while, then begins to twist and turn while gently sloping down. You notice offshoots going off in different directions, and in many places the tunnel forks, forcing you to choose a direction. Very quickly you realise you are lost in a maze!

Pausing to calm yourself, you reflect that at least things can not get worse - when a sudden gust of wind blows out the torch in your hand, and the shock of it makes you drop the torch. You are lost in a maze, in pitch black, and no-one knows you are there. As your eyes get used to the dark, you notice a faint glow a little further down the tunnel, so you walk toward it, carefully stepping on the uneven floor of the tunnel. You round a bend, to find yourself confronted by a large lioness standing in a glowing sphere of light. She is looking straight at you, and a small growl comes from her mouth as she displays her sharp teeth.

Fear takes hold of you, and you are about to turn and run when you realise that the light is emanating from the lioness. You look closer at her, and see wisdom and love in her eyes, so instead of fleeing, you walk cautiously towards her, entering the pool of ethereal light.

Reaching her side, you gingerly touch her hide, and she purrs quietly at you, calming your fears. She begins to walk down the tunnel, and you walk beside her as she turns left and right, you stay in her sphere of light, sensing that no harm will come to you.

Before long, you see another light ahead, and realise that she has led you back to the entrance. She stops and motions you onward, so you continue alone to the exit, turning at the end to see, not a lioness, but a beautiful woman in red, who says to you, "When you are ready to walk to the end of my path, come this way again, and I will guide thee."

With that, she vanishes into the darkness, and you turn and step into the sunlight, now that the storm has passed. Realising that the lioness was an aspect of Sekhmet, you silently thank her for her help, before returning to your home. The journey is ended....for now.

MEDITATION

1. In the darkest corner of the Temple I feel Thy breath upon my neck, and knowledge of the danger of Thee is mine. Gracious Lady, I ask Thee that Thou sharest Thy essence with me, for though I be a servant of Un-Nefer, yet do I serve Thee also.

2. Show me Thy Magick, Great Lion Goddess, for I am Thy child, and she whom I love is Thine also. Part the

veil that I may see Thee, and know Thee, and love Thee.

3. Strong is She, mighty in Her Power, and the earth doth tremble at Her roar. "I am She", saith the Great Goddess, " and My hunger for the joys of life shall never cease. To be one with Me must thou give thyself to me, for I take what I will, and devour that which is not freely given unto me.

4. I am a savage Goddess, yet also am I a Goddess of great passion, and compassion. Love Me, and do honour unto Me, and I will heal thy wounds and teach thee My ways. Thou keepest My shrine, but thou spillest no wine to Me. Do this act in My name, and I will be one with thee when thou callest Me, and none may stand against thee.

5. In My name, heal, in My name teach, and I will show unto thee the secrets of the universe. Do not think, frail mortal, that I seek to steal thee from thy Lord, the Sacred One, for I will find Mine own followers. But thou canst serve Me in serving thy master, and the greater will be thy glory for the doing of it.

6. "Love me, AFNA, and fear me not, for I am of thee, and thou of Me. Thou art Priest of Sekhmet, and Priest of Asar, and shall thou be priest of many more, e're thy day is done. Learn thy lessons well, little one, for the Two Lands have need of thee and thine."

7. A sensual warmth envelopes my soul, and when it clears do I find myself alone, and the journey is ended.

Ptah

11. PTAH

Another ancient deity is Ptah, the Architect God, who has remained essentially unchanged since the first dynasty (c. 3000 BC): he is depicted as a man in tight-fitting linen wrappings wearing a high collar and a skull cap. He carries a sceptre known as a Was, composed of a staff with the ankh and Djed column combined as its headpiece.

As with many other deities, his temple taught a version of the creation that was centred around him, but their creation myth was unusual in that Ptah is said to give birth to Atum, after speaking the universe into existence. Here, Atum and the ennead he creates are conceived as the teeth and lips of Ptah, created by his heart (the seat of his intellect) and tongue. To achieve this creation, Ptah is joined with the Void as personified by Nun, to become Ptah-Nun, the "Father who begot Atum".

He was called Ptah Nefer-Her "Beautiful of Face", and his face was made of gold. His intermediary was the sacred bull, Apis, and a real bull was kept in Ptah's temple at Memphis as the living representation of Apis. His wife was Sekhmet and his son was Nefertum, who was later usurped by Imhotep, god of medicine.

Ptah was regarded as the supreme deity by the craftsmen of Egypt, who considered him to have created the skills of all sculpture and design. His High Priest was known as Wer Kherep Hemut, "Supreme Leader of Craftsmanship". Ptah was believed to mould the body of each newborn pharaoh out of purest electrum (an amalgam of gold and silver), and his limbs out of copper and iron: in particular, Ptah was the patron deity of the metalworkers. He stood unique among the major Egyptian deities in that he could be approached by anyone, rather than just by his own followers. Small shrines or kiosks were set up for this very purpose - and for this reason he was known as "The Ear which Hears".

For modern students, particularly those interested in Freemasonry, Ptah is primarily the Great Architect. It is he who put into motion the machinery of the universe, who built the Earth, who taught man the mysteries of architecture. He is found in Yesod, the Sphere of the Astral Plane, where all things that are to exist in the physical realm are first formed. This Sphere is known as the Foundation: all material things and events have their foundation on this level, and it is here that Ptah can best use his abilities to continue the work of creation according to his Master Plan, the Architect's blueprint for the whole of creation. The creation legend of Memphis is to some extent politically motivated, but does contain an element of truth: since Ptah is the embodiment of the Great Work in action - the blueprint as it were, then it is possible to say that Atum comes as much from the blueprint as the blueprint comes from Atum. This makes Ptah very ancient, possibly as old as Sekhmet herself.

Ptah's name gives us 5 in the old system, and this shows his concern with the material realm, rebuilding what his wife Sekhmet tears down in the endless cycle of life. In the new system he comes to 9, equating to power, the sphere of Yesod, and the perfect balance for the effect of Sekhmet (who also equals 9). Numerological analysis shows that Ptah is a surprisingly powerful deity, filled with the authority and justice that he needs to fulfill his vision. He is linked closely with the Sun, and lives to bring Order to the universe.

Ptah is another one of the "Old Gods". Dressed in his skullcap, with a high collar and figure-hugging clothing, he is usually depicted in deep blue with gold trim. His symbols are the sacred staff or sceptre, and the square and compass of Freemasonry. He is most often pictured standing in a small kiosk, much simpler than the shrines of other deities.

Ptah is a very straightforward deity. Working with him is like working with a good teacher or professor - he is calm, quiet, and always has the information at his fingertips, providing you stick to his area of expertise. In Ptah's case this is how things work and how to make them - both material and spiritual things. Take him outside this area, though, and his help becomes unreliable.

In Egypt he was seen as the commoner's friend, because unlike the other deities he could be approached directly by anyone without the intercession of a priest or priestess. He was even at some points treated as a sort of agony aunt, with peasants spilling out their woes in the hopes of a solution becoming evident, or even the problem going away, at the hand of the God.

When Masons speak of the Great Architect of the Universe, they are basically speaking of Ptah, despite the attempts to equate GAOTU - as he is called in their little blue books - to the Christian god in order to refute claims of paganism and devil-worship from the church. The greatest gift he can bestow on you is his Vision of the Mechanics of the Universe, but you don't have to be aware of him to receive it.

Many of the great breakthroughs in physics and chemistry can be attributed to Ptah, either directly or through the agency of Thoth, God of Science. Newton caught a glimpse of Ptah's vision, leading to his scientific discoveries - which he claimed were mere byproducts of his mystical studies.

Einstein was another who saw the universe through Ptah's eyes, as was Gallileo, Francis Bacon, and many others.

In modern times physicists have come up with the theories of Quantum Mechanics which provide the version of creation given in chapter two - Ptah's hand is seen more clearly here than anywhere else. If you work with Ptah, he will show you his vision, in a form relevant to your way of life and profession: he provided me with the vision for this book, though the words are inspired by Thoth.

PATHWORKING

Each of the chapters on the gods will have a section like this. It is a guided spiritual journey to encounter the deity in a way that will enhance your understanding of him or her. The journeys will have a spiritual effect on you that increases with each one you do. You can either do them in the order that they appear in the book, or follow the order of deities in the correspondence tables in appendix 3.

You will need to prepare yourself for the journey. Ideally, have someone there to read the journey to you, or record it on cassette, and play it back to yourself. Seat yourself in a comfortable chair, and take a few moments to get as comfortable as you can. Try not to cross your legs or arms as this is a defensive posture that will lessen your concentration.

After you have taken a few deep breaths, and you feel really comfortable, begin your tape or get your partner to read the journey to you. At the end of the journey, have a good stretch and a hot drink - in Ancient Egypt it was traditional to drink hot chocolate after spiritual work. Now for the journey itself.

You are walking towards the walls of a city, not yet complete. At its top workers apply plaster, while in other areas artists paint scenes of triumph and festivity. To one side is the gateway into this new city, busy with carts and workers, raising the dust as they go about their business.

Inside the gateway, to one side of the road, is a small kiosk containing a statue of Ptah. Many of the workers pause here to have a quiet word in the direction of this, the common man's God. Approaching the kiosk, you too decide to offer a small prayer to Ptah, but to your surprise, you find that the statue is not mere stone and paint, but the deity himself. Ptah of the Golden Face speaks to you.

"I have seen thee on thy travels, Seeker, and for thee do I have a message that is short and simple. Many desire to learn of the Mysteries, but just as a house without foundations will not survive the flood, so their efforts are wasted because they do not build their work on sound basics. Thou wouldst travel far on thy path, and thus must thou wear stout sandals, that they fail thee not."

"The sandals are the Sacred Ground on which thou treadest, and are seen in the Ankh that my Lady, Sekhmet doth bear." He then speaks to you of aspects of the Mysteries that interest or puzzle you, until with a smile he bids you return to your own realm, and your brief journey is over.

MEDITATION

1. Great Ptah, Builder of the Inner Temple, Architect of the Universe, I call on Thee. Speak to me of Thy Plan, and show me Thy ways, that I may understand Thee.

2. I stand in the Temple court, and see the priests that do dwell therein. The Mighty Lords in their robes of blue and gold do pass me as they go about their ways, and the lowly we'ebs do scurry about on their errands. Yet all is peaceful, for speech is in quiet whispers, and the sanctity of the land is evident. I enter the halls of the Temple.

3. He is there before me, the Ancient One of Memphis. In His cap of deepest blue I see the night sky, and to behold His form is to behold reality. Great Lord, grant me Thy wisdom.

4. He speaks. "Through the minds of men, and with forces out of Nature do I perform My works. Thou seest but a portion of that which thou callest the Universe, and yet still art thou awed by it. Mine is the Plan, Mine is the Work. I exist, that all else may exist by the work of My hands. Seekest thou to be of service unto me? Then follow thou that plan which is allotted unto thee. Serve thy Lord and Mine, and seek not to hide behind hesitation and uncertainty, for thou knowest the truth, that thou art the one to do this Work.

5. "For reason hast thou been called "Prophet" by My Brethren, the Company of the Gods. Thou hast forged a True Link. Now must thou use that link, and step forth into thy world as a bringer of wisdom, a Teacher of the Mysteries. Thou art sent, not as saviour, nor as leader, but to instruct as one man teacheth another, in True Brotherhood. In the teaching of others shalt thou learn in Truth, and thy disciples will be Strong and True in the ways of Khem, for thus it is written upon the Great Plan that I do possess.

6. "Thy teacher, Amenemta, hast taken his turn as Prophet of the Gods, and hath returned at thy request to teach thee. Now thou must go forth and teach students of thine own, for the Order that thou servest grows stronger, and thine adversaries grow also stronger.

7. "Love the Gods, and thy fellow initiates, and serve the Light." He turneth away, and once more am I alone with my thoughts.

Thoth

12. THOTH

Thoth: to those who know him, his name echoes through the corridors of time, taking on new sounds for new times. Hermes, Mercury, Merlin - his name and face may change, yet his essence remains the same. Thoth is the god presiding over all knowledge, keeper of the secrets of science, art and magic. As Lord of the Sacred Words, he gave the Egyptians their hieroglyphic writing, writing possessed of a magical force that touches even our sceptical society, millennia later. The scribes of Egypt referred to themselves as the Followers of Thoth, and were a privileged class indeed.

Thoth was the embodiment of all scientific and literary attainment, holding the Sacred Books in the House of Life (the Library of Alexandria, though originally a part of the Temple of Hathor at Dendera) under his command - a library only available to scribes which contained manuals on medicine, magic, law, science, and the arts. His mentality was said to be so advanced that of all the gods, only he had the power to understand the Creator in his entirety.

As Scribe of the Gods, it was Thoth's duty to record all the souls entering the Underworld, and the results of their test against the Feather of Truth. His knowledge was often called upon by other gods, and he always seemed willing to help if it was for the good; he helped Geb and Nut to conceive their children, Isis to conceive Horus, and he also helped to pacify Sekhmet.

To modern day occultists, Thoth is Keeper of the Akashic Record, and a deity to invoke for help in obtaining information, especially when that information is contained in a book or, for that matter, a computer. When the Greeks looked into the face of Thoth, they saw the majesty of their own Hermes magnified a hundredfold, and so they named him: Hermes Trismegistos, Thrice Greatest Hermes. They proclaimed him the inventor of all the sciences, including astrology, and the initiator and imparter of all Hermetic Wisdom. All the secrets of the universe are said to be written in the Seven Books of Thoth, and even the Tarot is attributed to him.

Thoth dwells in the Sphere of Hod, as the Perfect or Complete Intelligence. He is perhaps the most widely recognised deity from Egypt, as his influence spreads through the Hermetic Science into Alchemy, Gnostic Christianity, Freemasonry, and the many Rosicrucian Orders. Indeed, his symbol (the winged caduceus staff with two entwined serpents) is used even today to represent the medical profession.

The name Thoth comes to 6 in the old system and 8 in the new. Six gives us the Vision of the Harmony of Things, the rose cross, devotion to the Great Work, and the intellect. Eight gives us Hermes, Mercury, the Vision of Splendour, the masonic apron and truthfulness. Numerologically, Thoth is an also an 8. Lord of Time, he is a well-balanced being who tempers his warrior instincts with the authority and rulership of those about him - Ra and Osiris. But even this is not his limit - all the while he studies the secrets of the universe, the laws that govern both the seen and the unseen.

Thoth is a tall slim male with the head of an Ibis. He wears a kilt and sash, and is most often seen holding a stylus and block - the bic biro and notepad of Ancient Egypt. He may occasionally be seen in meditations as wholly human with an Ibis pendant. His symbols are the ibis, the baboon, and the writing implements mentioned above. The ibis represents the mind's ability to fly free and form concepts unlimited by the available facts, and also to probe for the grain of truth in the dross of the riverbed. The baboon represents man's intellect as an imperfect copy of Thoth's own mighty mind.

The writing implements are self-explanatory when you remember that Thoth invented writing, and perhaps the best way to work with Thoth is through the medium of the written word. Any modern equivalent, ink pen, typewriter, wordprocessor, will evoke the influence of Thoth if you let it. He is the author's inspiration, the poet's muse, the journalist's literary skill.

To work with Thoth is to feel the touch of true wisdom. It is his will that man should know all things, but only as he becomes ready to accept them. Thoth will aid you in your studies, and will teach you of the ways of the Temple. He is kind and patient as a teacher, like an elderly uncle who delights in your interest of his hobby. He has great skills in diplomacy and politics: if you have to speak in public, let his influence aid you. As Lord of Truth, he will not help you to deceive, but his presence overshadowing you may enable you to persuade others that what you say is true.

He is traditionally the keeper of the Great Book in which he writes every event, and he will help you in a just cause, providing you accept the outcome, whatever it is. Above all, he is a father-figure.

PATHWORKING

Each of the chapters on the gods will have a section like this. It is a guided spiritual journey to encounter the deity in a way that will enhance your understanding of him or her. The journeys will have a spiritual effect on you that increases with each one you do. You can either do them in the order that they appear in the book, or follow the order of deities in the correspondence tables in appendix 3.

You will need to prepare yourself for the journey. Ideally, have someone there to read the journey to you, or record it on cassette, and play it back to yourself. Seat yourself in a comfortable chair, and take a few moments to get as comfortable as you can. Try not to cross your legs or arms as this is a defensive posture that will lessen your concentration. After you have taken a few deep breaths, and you feel really comfortable, begin your tape or get your partner to read the journey to you. At the end of the journey, have a good stretch and a hot drink - in Ancient Egypt it was traditional to drink hot chocolate after spiritual work. Now for the journey itself.

Standing just inside the entrance to a large Temple, you can see no one, but the scratching of a stylus on papyrus tells you that someone is there, so you walk among the many columns, looking for the source of the sound. After a short while, you come upon an elderly scribe, writing slowly and carefully on a tattered sheet of papyrus. He appears to be copying something from the base of a column, but as you come closer, he stops and looks up at you.

"What are you doing here?" he asks, and you tell him that you are seeking the wisdom of Thoth. He laughs, and says, "then gaze upon the wisdom of Thoth", and holds out the papyrus on which he has been working. You see that he has not been copying an inscription, but must have been following instructions inscribed on the column, for he has drawn a picture of an ibis on a crocodile's back, surrounded by a serpent with its tail in its mouth. Upon the serpent's body you see symbols. Some, such as the Square and Compass, and the Pyramid, are familiar, but the others are strange to you, and as you stare at them they seem to spin as if the snake were revolving around the crocodile and ibis.

All goes misty, and you find yourself standing before a tall young man, who has an ibis pendant about his neck, and a baboon sitting at his feet. The Temple in which you stand is the same one, but the colours are brighter, and the artwork is obviously new. Thoth takes the papyrus from your hand and bids you sit with him. Now is the time to ask questions of Thoth, for in matters of your studies, both esoteric and mundane, he will help you to find the answers. Take your time, and when you have finished, bid him farewell, and return to your own home, and the journey is over. (Please allow a space in any tape recording of this pathworking for the questions and answers, and then make sure you record instructions to return to your conscious self.)

MEDITATION

1. Lord of the Secret Word, Master of the Sacred Book, I stand here before Thee in the hopes of a glimpse of Thy Work. Reveal Thyself unto me, Noble One, for I would learn from Thee.

2. Thou who art the Ruler of All the Sciences, hear my words. I have felt Thy hand upon me, and I would know more of Thee. Speak Thou unto my soul, and fill me with Thy Wisdom.

3. The Sacred Ibis wades near the bank of the Nile, searching for its food. To my side do I see one of the Temple apes, a baboon of curious dignity, eating also. As I sit, I gaze upon the incomprehendable papyrus that doth lie before me. "Master," saith I, " I cannot read these words, for they are strange."

4. "Read them not with thine eyes, foolish child," saith the Master gently, " but with thy heart, for it is there that thou will find the meanings of this text." I look once more at the script, and tears well up into my eyes as I perceive the beauty and wisdom of the ancient writings. "Truly, thou art wise, O Master, for behold, the words are now plain to me, and their beauty is wondrous."

5. "In truth, Little One, hast thou learnt a great lesson this day, for unless thou canst feel the words in thine heart, they are but leaves blown by the wind. But when thy heart calls out to them, the words transform, and become as seeds to grow in the fertile soil of thine intellect, and thus art thou thrice blessed; for to read the words of a wise man is a blessing of thy circumstance, and to hear his thoughts in thy mind is a blessing of education. But to feel his joy and his wonder at the marvels of the universe is a true blessing indeed, for then art thou wise thyself!"

6. Then do I perceive that I do stand before the Scribe of the Gods, and awe of Him overcomes me. "Yes," saith He, "that vision was of thee as thou wert in the days of the Glory of Khem. As a young student of the Temple, thou ever bemoaned your abilities, until that day that thou hast even now observed, when thou took the Great Lesson to thy heart, and grew to be a great High Priest in the Temple of thy Master. Remember this, O Little One, for thou must teach it now to thine own wailing students." And with a wave of His hand, He departeth to His Sacred Book, and I continue mine Inner journey.

13. RA

Ra, the King of the Gods. The very name invokes a feeling of awe and majesty. Ra is the ultimate solar deity in the Egyptian Mysteries, being the source of all manifestations of the sun god in all three realms of sky, earth, and the Underworld. His many-fold nature is typified by his title "the One God in 120 Forms". Ra himself is often depicted as a falcon-headed man, wearing a headdress made up of a solar disk surrounded by a cobra. In the Underworld he is depicted as a ram-headed god, and during the different parts of the day he appears in different forms; as Khepera the scarab in the morning, as Ra himself at noon, and as Tem, an old man with gold skin and silver bones, in the evening.

Mankind is said to have been formed from the tears of Ra. The Egyptian word for tears, Remy, is very similar to the word for mankind, Remet. The relationship between Ra and the pharaohs began in the Fifth Dynasty, and from that time on all pharaohs received the title "Son of Ra" upon their coronation. Many royal temples were built in honour of Ra, and the pyramids themselves were designed to represent the primordial mound from which Ra rose at the dawn of time, and from which he rises every morning.

By the Twelfth Dynasty, the Egyptian initiates had evolved the concept of Ra and Osiris being united in a single form. They called this form "Ra in Osiris, Osiris in Ra". This played a vital part in the Inner Mysteries, and in the initiation to these Mysteries the postulant, after being tested, was informed;

Ra

"These two gods which are so dissimilar...[that they] seem to be opposites... are indeed one and the same." Called the "Reunited Soul", this deity was shown as a mummy wrapped in a ram's skin, and in contemplating it the new adept was reunited with his own spirit and entered on the path of Higher Magick; for the message is that death and life are not simply related - they are the same thing.

In the creation myth, Ra arose from the Nun (the primordial ocean, or Void) as a child in a lotus flower, upon the primordial mound. It is from this mound that he rises each morning in his sun boat, and this beautiful image deserves at least a mention. Each dawn, Ra rises from the mound as Khepera, the scarab god, in his sun boat. By noon, as he travels across the sky, he assumes the form of Ra the falcon god, and by evening he has transformed himself into Tem, the old and frail king. At sunset the boat enters the underworld, through which it travels until the new dawn when he emerges as Khepera once more.

The three forms of the solar god from sunrise to sunset can be better understood by thinking like an equatorial farmer: Khepera, the morning sun, is cool and was thought of as the nourishing, replenishing ray that made the plants grow. Ra, the noonday sun, is so powerful that it could wither those same plants, and kill men with its heat: and Tem, the setting sun, is old and feeble but beautiful in the memory of its lost glory.

Ra resides in Kether, the Primordial Point, and is a direct manifestation of Atum on the higher planes of creation. In the new numerical system Ra comes to 1, which is of course the number of the sun. One represents brilliance, union with god, the elixir of life, and the roots of all elemental powers. Through numerology, Ra comes across as someone with great power and magic coupled with leadership and authority. He is definitely the Manifestation of Atum that his legend suggests.

Great Ra, Lord of Light, has several common forms and many less common ones. For practical purposes we shall concentrate on the form he assumes at noonday, when he is Ra-in-His-Boat. Wearing a white kilt and golden collar, his head is that of a falcon topped by the solar disk or the horned Atef Crown. He is usually depicted on his Solar Boat, manned by the other gods and with the solar disc, Aten, upon its bow. His symbols are the solar disc, the Sun Boat, the scarab and the pyramid. All of these have a place in his legend and are self-explanatory.

Ra is aloof and distant, much as you would expect a king to be, but behind his formality is a love of humanity that helps to temper his stern and powerful countenance. Once you get to know him, he seems more like a father, and he will always encourage your efforts. As a solar deity, he is concerned with good fortune and wealth, and he is a good deity to call upon to help in business affairs - provided they are performed honourably. Working with him will give you a sense of confidence, and an inner glow that will help others to have confidence in you.

When called upon for purposes of protection of a person, he is very effective, but can go beyond what was intended - if you call on him to protect your sister, for example, and her husband is not good for her he will cause the husband to leave - so definite goals and limitations must be employed when working with Ra.

In his alternate form of Khepri, the Scarab, he is an excellent deity to place over the start of a new project, as Khepri is the God of Beginnings. He is much more distant in this aspect, though, so call on the Ra aspect first, and ask him to transform when you have explained your requirements, to help communication.

PATHWORKING

Each of the chapters on the gods will have a section like this. It is a guided spiritual journey to encounter the deity in a way that will enhance your understanding of him or her. The journeys will have a spiritual effect on you that increases with each one you do. You can either do them in the order that they appear in the book, or follow the order of deities in the correspondence tables in appendix 3.

You will need to prepare yourself for the journey. Ideally, have someone there to read the journey to you, or record it on cassette, and play it back to yourself. Seat yourself in a comfortable chair, and take a few moments to get as comfortable as you can. Try not to cross your legs or arms as this is a defensive posture that will lessen your concentration.

After you have taken a few deep breaths, and you feel really comfortable, begin your tape or get your partner to read the journey to you. At the end of the journey, have a good stretch and a hot drink - in Ancient Egypt it was traditional to drink hot chocolate after spiritual work. Now for the journey itself.

You find yourself in darkness. You can see nothing, but realise that you are standing in a boat from the motion of the waves. The total absence of light tells you that the boat is floating on the Waters of the Nun, the primordial nothingness out of which all came forth.

Ahead of you a faint glow appears, revealing the silhouette of a pyramid-shaped mound, and you watch as the source of light rises up from behind or within the mound. As it reaches the summit, you see that it is a brilliant solar disk, carried by a giant Scarab, and you realise that you are witnessing the dawn of the day. As the solar disk rises higher, you see that the image has transformed, and the Sun Disk is now affixed to the bow of a boat, upon which stands the majestic figure of Ra. He looks toward you and suddenly you find yourself standing beside him on the deck of the Solar Boat.

The Boat reaches the peak of its arc, and begins to descend, and you watch as the majestic figure beside you changes once more, becoming wholly human in appearance, and then ageing, until the moment when the Boat comes to ground at the Place of Sunset, when Ra, in his form of Tem, is ancient and weak.

The boat begins to descend into the mound, and suddenly you find yourself back in your own boat, watching Ra descend into the Tuat, and your short journey is over.

MEDITATION

1. Behold, the Light of the Great God descends once more, and I am enflamed with the glory thereof. My heart is Thine, O Osiris, and Thy Will is my purpose in life, for Thou art the Giver and the Taker of all things upon the earth.

2. The sound of birdsong fills my head as I look about me. All around is the purest of nature's work, the rocks, and the sand, and the hawks. Alone I stand upon a rocky outcrop, glorying in the radiance given forth by He of the Double Horizon, Great Ra-in-His-Boat. I turn at a sound, and see the glory of the Great God beside me, and the Voice of the Sun, which saith:

3. "Great is thy faith, O Prophet, and many are the works to be done by thee. Hearest thou the call of the hawk? He is like unto the Solar Disk, my strength and power, for in his golden brilliance and smooth contours hideth a multitude of sinews and fibres that will not yield to those that are unworthy. Likewise are My secrets hidden by the radiance that shineth forth from my countenance. But look thou carefully behind the glare, with eyes set so as to cut out that which conceals, and thou shalt see for thyself that which the Divine Hawk of Light doth possess. Even my Right Eye, that poureth forth good things, shall be known unto he who dares to look through the glare and heat of ignorance and time, and my Left Eye shall hold no power over him, save at the Time of Reckoning, when He who ruleth the Two Lands calleth for the Scales to be brought forth.

4. For unto that man shall be given the power of Light and Truth, and he shall be as one with the gods, a Follower of Horus, and beloved of Ra. If thou wouldst come unto the Great Hall as a God, then must thou look upon Me as thou would thine own reflection, and see thyself in my Sacred Face, and know that I am within thyself. The one to whom this power is given shall not fear any man, but trust in the Greater Company of Gods, be he Pharaoh or be he the poorest beggar beside the gates of the Temple.

5. Thus do I say unto thee, that thou must follow the words of the Brothers and learn well their secrets, that thou mayest gaze even upon Mine Own Face and there see thyself enthroned in glory and purity. Therefore, let thou seek the true teachings, even those passed down from my ancient time to thine, and give thy knowledge freely to those who seek it.

6. And let not thy mortal weakness and frailty tempt thee to fail, for true pursuit of this task is all that is open to thee. Let not the mocking words of vulgar fools steer thee in the ways of the masses, but tread thou steadfast upon the path thou cravest above all others.

7. With this I shall depart, but remember that the True Way lies within thee, as it doth in all men. Thou must search for it, and pay thy way with a sharing of thy new knowledge, and the heights of attainment shall be thine.

8. Farewell, Prophet. Be thou mindful of the Old and the New." saith the Lord of Light. Then doth He depart, and all is darkness, save only that light which issueth forth from the Silver Disk of the Moon.

14. ASAR-RA

The name of Asar-Ra very probably fails to evoke even a glimmer of recognition in the mind of you, the reader. Unless you are fond of digging through the more obscure passages of the Book of the Dead, or perhaps some of the magical papyri, it is unlikely that you will ever have heard of Asar-Ra before opening this book. There is no doubt that the initiates of the Inner Temple made use of such a deity, but you will not find him mentioned in any popular work, with the single exception of C Jacq's "Egyptian Magic". And why? Because his existence was only known to the High Priests and senior adepts of the Temples, and according to the occult theory of secrecy, this made him extremely powerful.

As the name implies, Asar-Ra is the entity known as "Ra in Osiris, Osiris in Ra" mentioned in the chapter on Ra himself. On a basic level, he has many similarities with Atum, being considered as a manifestation into this universe of the Creator: at an esoteric level however there are a great differences. Atum is seen as the Self-Created Light, but Asar-Ra is a subtler form, the Uncreated Light, which was said in the legends to have manifested separately as Ra and Osiris in order to be more accessible to lesser minds such as the human race. It was Asar-Ra who told Hap, the God of the Nile, exactly when to open the floodgates to cause the annual inundation, and it is he who newly-initiated adepts were shown in the form of a mummy wrapped in a ram skin.

Asar-Ra can be depicted in several ways. His most common form - and even that is rare - is of a mummified body with the falcon head of Ra and the White Crown of Osiris, complete with plumes. At Abydos, he is represented in the

Asar-Ra

form of Ra-Herakhti (his mundane name) in the reliefs, but almost every other representation of him is in the magical papyrae. Despite all this secrecy, one single reference to him has reached the modern western world. In MacKenzie's *Royal Masonic Cyclopaedia* - one of the books that inspired the founders of the Golden Dawn - there is an entry for the College of Six. This was, according to the book, the ruling body of the Egyptian Mysteries, and was founded by Ases-Ra.

An inner group of the highes adepts was known as the "College of Six". This was the Ptolemaic title of what was originally called the "Company of Nine" - the decline of the number of Adepts must have necessitated a renaming. This council, consisting of the eight greatest adepts plus the Pharaoh as nominal head, was the governing body of the Inner Mysteries, which was known as the Four Orders because there were four grades of Priesthood. It was said by Greek historians that of all the temples of Egypt, there was not one where the senior priests were not members of the Four Orders. Please note that the words priest and priesthood as I have used them here include the priestesses, who were accorded equal (and frequently senior) status to their male counterparts. Asar-Ra represents the masculine elements of the entire life cycle. His ideal female counterpart is the Twin Cobra Goddess, Isis-Nephthys, covering the feminine elements of the life cycle - although for magical reasons he is sometimes partnered with Sekhmet.

The magical system worked by the Sacred Hermetic Order of Asar-Ra pays a great deal of attention to this deity, as their name suggests. He is seen as the personification of the supreme Creator, with all other gods being aspects of him. This does not prevent the initiates of the Order from using the better-known deities, but rather enables them to use different godforms without losing a sense of unity with each other. In much the same way that a catholic will pray to the appropriate saint for a particular problem rather than to Jehovah, so the S.H.O.A.R. initiate uses a particular deity as the relevant aspect of the Creator to deal with the problem.

The name Asar-Ra comes to 13 in the old system and 22 in the new. Both add to four, which gives; Amun (the "Hidden One"), the Vision of Love, the wand, the sceptre and crook, the pyramid, all good things, and the Brilliant One. Thirteen itself gives the Uniting Intelligence, contentment, and the Priestess of the Silver Star. Twenty-two gives justice, Maat, and works of justice and equilibrium. Numerologically, Asar-Ra gives 22, the most spiritually exalted number possible. Such a being has much love and inner power, and is the embodiment of all the solar deities on every level. This is the number that makes numerologists jump!

Asar-Ra is very rarely depicted in Egyptian art. In fact, the only reference to his appearance describes him as being represented by a mummy draped with a ram's skin, complete with horns. Having said this, he does have a definite image. He is seen as a hawk-headed man wrapped in mummy wrappings, wearing the horned Atef Crown on the front of which is the Solar Disk. In his hands, which extend out of the wrappings, are the Crook, the Flail, and the Ur Hekau, or Rod of Power. Sometimes the twin souls of Osiris and Ra are shown as hawks in the correct headdresses, upon his shoulders. He is always attended by four cloaked figures who are the prototypes of the Sons of Horus, and are known as the Noble Lords of the Quarters.

Contacting Asar-Ra is hard work, for his realm is in a region rarely visited by mortal minds, and visits to him are necessarily short. He gives a strong impression of limitless power, and also supreme authority. If you visit him, be sure to have a good reason for although he does not punish anyone if your reason is spurious, you will find yourself alone in your physical self, and you will not be able to work with the archetypes again until you have had a good night's sleep. This is a deity that does not waste time. Normally, you would only work with Asar-Ra for things to do with your spiritual progress, but he will turn his attention to mundane matters that have a bearing on or affect spiritual matters. His usual contribution is to advise you on a course of action that will enable you to sort things out for yourself.

Because of the nature of the Deity, there is no set pathworking in this chapter. Rather, once you have completed all of the other pathworkings in the book, visualise yourself in the sanctuary of one of the Egyptian Temples, and see a spiral of gold marked on the floor. Stand in the centre of the spiral, and feel yourself travelling in some strange direction. If you are ready, you will encounter Asar-Ra, but if not, you will merely return to your starting point.

MEDITATION

1. Great Asar-Ra, Thou Uncreated Light, I would ask a word from Thee. Let me see Thy Splendour, that I may tell of Thee and teach Thy ways.

2. Radiant is He, the Lord of All. In His realm I stand, and barely can I maintain myself in this place. Then doth He touch my shoulder, and all is calm, and I am at ease.

3. "For but a short time may thou remain here," He saith, "for this realm was not for mortals made. I will speak unto thee and tell thee of Mine own Self, for thus do thou wish it to be.

4. "I am He Who is Both the Day and the Night. In me do the Great Twin Souls reside, and I am All-Powerful. Mine is the Sacred Land, and that which is above, and that which is beneath. Neither desert storm nor the wiles of man may take from Me that which is Mine, and though the whole world perish, yet shall I remain.

5. "I am the Midnight Sun, and My radiance doth illuminate the darkest of places. To the Forces of Chaos I do say, Get ye back to your despised realms, for there is no resting place for you here. To My children do I say, Peace unto ye all, for in this Age of the Heartlessness of Man are ye precious unto the Gods. My heart is sad at the ravages of soulless men, and My tears do wash the soil, but not enough.

6. "For thou must cry out, and restore the Sacred Work to the land. Khemi is no more, but thou canst build up a new Khemi in thy heart, that the world of mortal man may be saved. I will say no more, for thy visit here hath tired thee, and thou must return. Go now, and rest. Thy task for the moment is done. Rest, and awake refreshed that thou may complete the work. Farewell."

15. THE ANKH OF ASAR-RA

The Ankh of Asar-Ra is a symbol that you will not find in any tomb or temple of Ancient Egypt, although it does have a predecessor in the form of the Staff carried by Ptah. It consists of a golden Solar Disk surrounded by a Uraeus Serpent above the Tet of Osiris, which is flanked by the Wings of Isis. Upon the Solar disk is a hexagram, and upon the serpent are five disks representing five of the Spheres of the Tree of Life. The top of the Tet is a square representing a sixth Sphere, the tips of the wings contain two more, and the Tet itself has the last two, one half-way down, and one at the bottom. The Spheres can be shown in the Sephirotic colours or the godform colours, depending upon the use to which the Ankh is to be put.

Obviously the symbol is a synthesis of the gods Ra, Osiris, and Isis, but there is much more to it than that. The hexagram represents man's search for unity with the Creator, and the wisdom he gains along the way. The serpent is a symbol of both wisdom and protection, while the five disks on the serpent hint at the pentagram, symbol of man in harmony with the elements of nature. The Sphere of Tiphareth is represented by the square at the top of the Tet, where all the symbols come together - appropriate for the Sphere of Enlightenment. The wings symbolise protection, but also nurturing, and the ability to fly free. The Tet is the ladder of seven degrees leading to adept status: S.H.O.A.R. does not initiate beyond seventh degree, although it recognises ten degrees.

As a whole, the Ankh of Asar-Ra symbolises the Hidden Wisdom that can only be found when the separate elements of the Mysteries are viewed as a whole. Too many modern

Ankh of Asar-Ra

practitioners of Egyptian Magic find an affinity with one deity and work with that god to the exclusion of all the others. This does not give a balanced picture to the Mysteries, and leads to rivalry of the "my god is bigger than your god" variety which started Christianity and Islam on their present exclusivist course.

In S.H.O.A.R, the students do work with a patron deity once they are advanced enough to be able to choose one (or be chosen by one!), but before they reach that stage, they work on experiencing as many deities as they can, and throughout their spiritual evolution they work with the whole range, their patron deity being there for tuition and personal protection.

The Ankh, known as the Egyptian Cross, and sometimes - if incorrectly - as the Tau Cross, is a symbol that conjures up Ancient Egypt in an instant. As a hieroglyph, it was used in two ways. Pronounced as ONKH it meant "key", and pronounced "ANKH" it meant "Life". From this it gained its commonly accepted interpretation of "Key of Life" or "Tree of Life".

The standard ankh consists of two parts, a Tau Cross ("T"-shape) and a circle. The Tau consists of a central square with three arms, each containing three squares. This gives ten squares that are traditionally attributed to the spheres of the Qabalistic Tree of Life.

The circle, shown as a ring, consists of the centre, the inner boundary of the ring, and the outer boundary. To continue the Qabalistic correspondence, theses can be equated to the VOID, the LIMITLESS, and the LIMITLESS LIGHT. The Void, Ain in Hebrew, is in the Egyptian system the Nun, the primordial waters of chaos from which all sprang.

The Limitless, Ain Soph in Hebrew, is Atum, the Creator, self-formed, who united with the Nun to bring forth the manifest Universe. This is a condition where there is no limit by time and space, and there is infinite potential.

The Limitless Light is the Manifest Universe at its moment of creation, and sees the Creator manifest within His creation as Ra. It is the Big Bang that started this universe with its concepts of time and space.

Another way of looking at these three "veils" is to see the void as Ra, the Limitless as Osiris, and the Limitless Light as Horus. Ra, as an aspect of the Creator is seen as distant and unapproachable. He sent Osiris as the First Manifestation of God among mortals, although he is not a complete manifestation until he undergoes his resurrection. He was the first mediator to teach humans the ways of the Divine.

Horus, son of Osiris, is seen as the incarnation of Ra, as the Solar Logos, a warrior placed in our world to combat the negative forces.

Tree of Life

It is possible to place the Tree of Life upon the entire Ankh, in a simplified form of the Ankh of Asar-Ra. Examples in the form of a Jewelled Ankh has been found in several tombs. But what can the ankh be used for in modern times?

The Ankh is an easily used key for meditation or astral travel to the Spiritual Land of Khem. For this reason, among others, it is seen as the Key to the Mysteries, and is often seen in the hands of deities symbolising the gift of Light, or Illumination. There is a secret to this, though.

In some pictures, the deity is shown holding two Ankhs. This is to tell the reader that there is a hidden meaning to the accompanying text, in addition to the obvious one.

An iron ankh representing life and a stylised snake representing wisdom were used in the Ritual of the Opening of the Mouth, and by priests invoking a deity. Meditating on the Ankh, or doing a pathworking using it as a gate, will teach you much about it and yourself. Try using a plain ankh, and then move on to the Ankh of Asar-Ra.

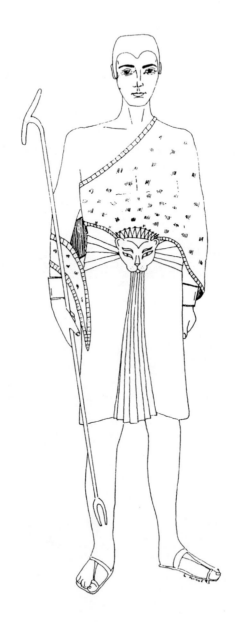

Ancient Egyptian Priest

16. THE EGYPTIAN QABALAH

I will say: "I know the numbers of my fingers". The Ferryman says: "Count, so that you may let me hear."

"Take the ONE, take the DOUBLE one, QUENCH it, REMOVE it, GIVE to me, what is JUDGED for me, LET IT GO, UNITE it, ILLUMINATE the Eye, give the EYE to me."

The priests of Ancient Egypt used puns on words to both hide and to reveal great mysteries, as discussed in the introductory chapter. The above passage, regarded by some as the source of the numerical Qabalah, must be dealt with in this way to coax its secrets into the open - each of the words and phrases in capitals is, in Egyptian, a pun on the word for the number. These ten numbers correspond to the ten Spheres of the Tree of Life, although the numerical values are reversed.

One, in Egyptian, is UA, and this also means the east bank of the Nile - the bank on which the people lived their lives - and is the name for the Mummy case, the physical remains of the departed soul. This equates with Malkuth, the material world on the Tree of Life. UA also means doorway, region, and Festival, showing that it is the region where the practices of the Festivals provide a doorway to what is beyond. It means document, the start of a journey, a peasant, to place in position, a bond, and to be about to do something. This suggests a person bound in place in (spiritual) poverty, who is about to begin a journey.

Two, in Egyptian, is SENUI. It means double in the sense of a copy or image. It corresponds to Yesod, the Sphere of Imagination, the Double. It also means chamber, offering, companion, and kiss. It is the chamber beyond the physical realm where true offerings can be made, and where the companion, or Guide for the Journey may be found. It has its negative aspects in its meanings of false, sufferer, failure, and misery, as none of these can function without the action of the mind.

Three is Khemt, and relates to Hod, the Sphere of Control. Khemt means provision and exclusion, that is, controlling what is and is not. It means dancers - with their bodily control, and the Ferryman, who controls the entry of souls into the realm of the gods.

Four, Aft, relates to Netzach, the Sphere of Attraction and Repulsion, of Energy. Aft means rest, a couch, and sarcophagus, which are all tools of astral projection, represented by another meaning of Aft, 'jump up from the ground'. It means 'sweat of the god', and this is how the legends relate that the Sons of Horus were created. Aft also means the Four Spirits. It is the realm of Duty, and the Bringer of the Eye of Horus.

Five, Tu, relates to Tiphareth, the Sphere of the Sun, and is the focus of man's essential nature. It is the Mountain, the dawn, and as such is represented by the rising of Ra at dawn from the Primeval Mountain. It means honour, and giving, and to arrive - it is a well-known fact that the initial goal of the Qabalist is to enter Tiphareth.

Six, Sas, is satisfaction through judgement, a trial, and to measure. All of these are attributes of the Sphere of Geburah. It means to exalt, and Prince, and Nobleman, and also 'to occupy a seat'. With the meanings of trial and offering, that seat could be the seat of judgement, but are you the judge, or the judged? Another meaning of the name Osiris is 'He who occupies the Throne'.

Seven, Skhef or Sefekh, relates to Chesed, inner emotions, and the creative urge. It is to unbind, to create, to write, also to undress, and to leave what is left. It is creativity in the sense of freeing the truth from that which restrains or conceals it.

Eight, Khemen, relates to Binah, understanding, and receptiveness. It means marriage, a water-course, approach, and to unite. It is also a title of Set, and this shows that the marriage concerned is that of the two sides of the self, the light and dark sides, separated by the flow of past events. It also means breathlessness, for continued existence in this realm is not automatic, but requires that your breath is provided by the gods, if you pass the test of the Ferryman.

Nine, Pest, means to shine, to illumine, ray of light, and 'the Nine Great Gods'. It relates to Chokmah, Sphere of Wisdom and the Inner Eye of Illumination.

Ten, Met, is the Phallus, man as creator, and the 'Emission of the God'. It relates to Kether, the first manifestation of the emission of Light from the Creator. It is the Centre, the Source, 'that which has always been', the Path of Heaven, and the Word. As the Path of Heaven, it is the end of the Path of Man, and the start of a new, unknown adventure.

In many of the Egyptian scriptures, the Path of Man consists of ten gates or Pylons, each guarded by a deity and two guardians, leading on to a further twenty-one gates, known as the Path of the God or the Path of the Heavens. The following table is a synopsis of some of the correspondences for the first ten gates.

GATE	SPHERE	DEGREE TITLE	DEITY
One	Malkuth	Master of the Door	Anubis
Two	Yesod	Master of the Earth	Ptah
Three	Hod	Master of the Hands	Thoth
Four	Netzach	Master of the Temple	Hathor/Sekhmet
Five	Tiphareth	Master of the Pyramid	Horus
Six	Geburah	Master of the Fire	Set & Nephthys
Seven	Chesed	Master of the Words	Osiris & Isis
Eight	Binah	Master of the Water-Course	Geb & Nut
Nine	Chokmah	Master of the Ray of Light	Shu & Tefnut
Ten	Kether	Master of the Universe	Ra/Atum

These ten gates were known as the "Path of Man", and there were another twenty-one gates called the "Gates of the God" that led back to the start again. The image used to portray these gates was of two disks interlocked at right angles to each other. The horizontal disk had ten rings, the vertical had twenty rings, and the circumferences were considered to be the final ring.

The thirty rings so formed equate nicely with the thirty aethyrs of Enochian Magic, long considered to be closely linked with the Egyptian Gods. Each ring on the Path of Man gives access to two rings on the Path of the God, resulting in ten major steps, each consisting of three lesser steps.

This link between the Egyptian, Qabalistic, and Enochian systems is one that for centuries has been suspected, with little or no proof to verify it. Most attempts to reconcile the systems with each other have merely confused the issue further. This is only my own pet theory, but it seems to be so simple, that it deserves to be true! Intelligent use of the image of the disks will facilitate the conversion of information, rituals, and ideas from one system to another.

Obviously, there is a great deal of study to be done on this subject. For a start, the way the Egyptian Priesthood worked, the Emissions of the God would have been worked into a legend, and an analysis of that legend will provide further enlightenment. But all that must wait for another book, as both time and space are limited in this one!

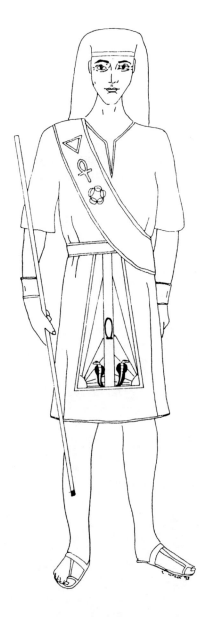

S.H.O.A.R. High Priest

17. CASTING AN EGYPTIAN CIRCLE

Anyone who has been taught about circle-casting and ritual construction can create their own Egyptian rites, but for those who are new to magick, or do not have the time to create their own rituals, I am including here the method of opening and closing the circle as used by S.H.O.A.R., and some guidelines on formulating a ritual.

It is important to remember that you should never perform a magickal act without first understanding why you are doing it and what it means. It may appear that I am stating the obvious, but if you look through the Greek Magical Papyrae, you will come across rites that seem safe, useful and are designed to do positive things, but which contain invocations to dark aspects of deities: such invocations could have grave repercussions on your life. Unless, that is, you know how to handle them.

Barbarous Words of Power are used in many ancient rites. These are not so much words as sonic vibrations that have profound psychological effects on our subconscious, and even greater magical effect on the Astral Plane. It is not a good idea to use them in your rites unless you have access to someone who can train you to intone them correctly and warn you of probable effects. For all practical purposes, the names of the deities, properly vibrated and projected, will more than suffice.

This, then, is the script of the S.H.O.A.R. Lodge Ritual in full. After it you will find an explanation of all parts of it. It is written to be performed by four people, conventionally referred to as officers of the quarters, but can be performed by two, or even by solo practitioners. If more than four people take part, then the extras are non-speaking participants, but should still actively participate by willing their energies to the speakers. They may also join in when "So mote it be" is said.

Officer of the North silently draws the circle three times with sword, dagger or fingers, visualising a line of blue light streaming forth as he/she does so. He/she then opens portal and admits the others, if any.

Officer of the North: (Osiris Litany) PRAISE AND SONGS OF GLORY UNTO THEE, O OSIRIS, UN-NEFER, LORD OF THE HIDDEN PLACE, WHOSE FORM IS MAJESTIC. BE THOU IN MY HEART, O BRINGER OF HARVEST, AND INSPIRE THOU ME TO WORKS OF TRUTH AND BEAUTY IN THINE HONOUR. GREAT IS THY FORM, AND WISE ARE THY WORDS, O LORD OF THE TWO RIVERS. THY SERVANT WAITETH, AND IS BUT AN EMPTY VESSEL TO BE FILLED WITH THY LUMINESCENCE. BREATHE THOU INTO HIM THAT DIVINE INSPIRATION THAT CAUSETH THE EARTH TO ROCK ON ITS FOUNDATIONS, O THOU WHO ART ENDLESS LIGHT.

(Isis Litany) IN THE BEAUTY OF THE NIGHT SKY I BEHOLD THEE, O ISIS, AND MY HEART IS LIGHT WITH THY PRESENCE. O THOU WHO ART CONSORT TO THY BROTHER, THE LORD OF ALL, I DO BOW TO THY BEAUTY, AND HONOUR THEE WITH EVERY ACT OF LOVE. QUIETLY AS A LARK'S WHISPER TO THE SETTING SUN DO I HEAR THY WORDS IN MY MIND, FAIR GODDESS, AND MY VERY SOUL IS FILLED WITH RAPTURE AT THY TOUCH. BE THOU THE GOVERNESS

OF MY EMOTIONS, THAT I MAY LOVE AND SERVE THEE AND THY HUSBAND, OSIRIS OF THE ONE FACE, WITH THE PURITY OF PERFECT TRUTH.

All face East

Officer of the East: MIGHTY QEBHSNUF, SON OF HORUS, LORD OF AIR, WE DO GREET THEE AND ASK THY ATTENDANCE AND ASSISTANCE IN THIS RITE.

All: SO MOTE IT BE!

All face South

Officer of the South: MIGHTY DUAMUTEF, SON OF HORUS, LORD OF FIRE, WE DO GREET THEE AND ASK THY ATTENDANCE AND ASSISTANCE IN THIS RITE.

All: SO MOTE IT BE!

All face West

Officer of the West: MIGHTY IMSETY, SON OF HORUS, LORD OF WATER, WE DO GREET THEE AND ASK THY ATTENDANCE AND ASSISTANCE IN THIS RITE.

All: SO MOTE IT BE!

All face North

Officer of the North: MIGHTY HAPI, SON OF HORUS, LORD OF EARTH, WE DO GREET THEE AND ASK THY ATTENDANCE AND ASSISTANCE IN THIS RITE.

All: SO MOTE IT BE!

All face Altar.

Officer of the North: (Osiris invocation) HAIL, THOU LORD OF THE SACRED LANDS, THOU MAJESTIC ONE OF THE UNDERWORLD! STRENGTHEN THOU US ACCORDING AS THOU HAST STRENGTHENED THYSELF, AND SHOW THYSELF UPON THE EARTH, O THOU THAT RETURNEST AND WITHDRAWEST THYSELF, AND LET THY WILL BE DONE!

(Isis invocation) GREAT ISIS, BEHOLD, THY HANDMAIDEN WAITS FOR THY PRESENCE. MAKE HER THY GARMENT FOR A SHORT SPACE OF TIME. MAY THY BLOOD, AND THY POWERS, AND THY ENCHANTMENTS BE IN HER, THAT SHE MAY DO THY WORK IN THIS PLACE.

Officer of the East: (Osiris invocation) BEHOLD, THE GOD OF ONE FACE IS WITH ME. I AM THE HAWK THAT IS WITHIN THE SHRINE, AND I OPEN THAT WHICH IS UPON THE HANGINGS THEREOF. BEHOLD OSIRIS, TRIUMPHANT IN GLORY!

(Isis invocation) I AM SHE WHO BORE THE CHILD HORUS! I AM SHE WHO KNOWS THE SECRET NAME OF RA. LEARN THE DEEPEST SECRET OF THIS UNIVERSE, AND YOU WILL FIND ME IN IT. THE QUEEN OF MAGICK IS AT THE HEART OF ALL THINGS, AND I AM SHE. BEHOLD ISIS, GREAT GODDESS OF MYSTERY!

Then follows any work to be done, followed by the Close.

Officer of the East: THE TIME HAS COME FOR AN ENDING - FOR ALL THINGS MUST END, THAT THERE MAY BE A NEW BEGINNING. BUT REMEMBER YE THIS - THE LIGHT OF THE TEMPLE BURNS IN THE HEART OF US ALL, THUS ARE WE ALL TEMPLES OF LIGHT AND MUST DEPORT OURSELVES ACCORDINGLY.

All face East

Officer of the East: MIGHTY QEBHSNUF, SON OF HORUS, LORD OF AIR, WE THANK THEE FOR THY PRESENCE,AND BID THEE RETURN TO THY ABODE IN PEACE.

All: SO MOTE IT BE!

All face South

Officer of the South: MIGHTY DUAMUTEF, SON OF HORUS, LORD OF FIRE, WE THANK THEE FOR THY PRESENCE AND BID THEE RETURN TO THY ABODE IN PEACE.

All: SO MOTE IT BE!

All face West

Officer of the West: MIGHTY IMSETY, SON OF HORUS, LORD OF WATER, WE THANK THEE FOR THY PRESENCE AND BID THEE DEPART TO THY ABODE IN PEACE.

All: SO MOTE IT BE!

All face North

Officer of the North: MIGHTY HAPI, SON OF HORUS, LORD OF EARTH, WE THANK THEE FOR THY PRESENCE AND BID THEE DEPART TO THY ABODE IN PEACE.

All: SO MOTE IT BE!

All face Altar

Officer of the North: ALL THAT HAS BEEN CREATED SHALL RETURN INTO THE NUN... MYSELF ALONE, I REMAIN, UNKNOWN, INVISIBLE TO ALL.

Officer of the East: IN THE NAME OF THE LORD OF ALL, I NOW SET FREE ANY SPIRITS THAT MAY HAVE BEEN TRAPPED BY THIS CEREMONY.

The Officer of the North claps his hands once.

Officer of the North: THE RITE IS ENDED!

All: SO MOTE IT BE!

PREPARATION

The circle is prepared with an altar, preferably square, in the centre. At each Quarter is a chair for the officer, with the Quarter candle to its left: seats for other participants may be placed around the perimeter of the room. The candle colours conform to the colours for the Sons of Horus as given below.

On the Altar should be two altar candles, an oil lamp and a representation of the deity to be worked with; either a statue, a picture, or the deity's symbol. Other relevant items may be added, but this is a comfortable minimum. The participants should all wear plain white robes with black cords if they are initiated, and white cords if they are not initiated into any system. Temple shoes are optional, but if worn, should be used exclusively for Egyptian rituals. Daggers should be worn on the cord if required.

THE LITANY

If the Officer of the East is male, the Osiris Litany and invocation are used; if female, the Isis litany and invocation are used. The litany is used for two purposes. Firstly, it helps to get everyone in the right frame of mind for the ritual, and gives a chance to calm down and open up. Secondly, it traditionally notifies the deity that he or she will be called upon, a sort of courtesy call. If deities other than Osiris or Isis are used you can write or find an appropriate litany to use, but for beginners and for most works of healing, learning and helping, Osiris and Isis will work perfectly well.

SONS OF HORUS

These are the Lords of the Four Quarters in the Egyptian System. In this rite they are placed in the quarters that S.H.O.A.R. associates them with, but different authorities give other placements. The table below gives the basic details needed for working with them;

Name	Pronounced	Element	Quarter	Head	Colour
Qebhsnuf	KWEBS-NUF	Air	East	Hawk	Blue
Duamutef	DOO-AMOO-TEF	Fire	South	Jackal	Red
Imsety	IMM-SETTEE	Water	West	Human	Green
Hapi	HAR-PEE	Earth	North	Baboon	Yellow

When you speak the words that summon one of the Sons of Horus, draw an invoking pentagram: either the pentagram of the relevant element, or the invoking earth pentagram illustrated - and visualise a kilted man with the appropriate head of the appropriate colour standing before you.

INVOCATION

Obviously, the invocation to match the initial litany is used. The invocation is in two parts, one said by the Officer of the North, and the other by the Officer of the East, who is the celebrant. All present should visualise the Officer of the East growing larger until he is so tall that the planet earth is a footstool on which he or she stands. They should then visualise him or her merging with the deity being invoked, and shrinking back down, bringing the deity into the circle, where the second part of the invocation is said to establish the presence of the deity.

THE WORK

In the temples of Ancient Egypt, most work was done using thought-forms, astral projection, and the spoken word. The use of wax effigies and talismans was more of a solo practice. The real key to the magick is visualisation, and the most basic - but still effective - form of visualisation is to picture the relevant deity supervising an event where the desired outcome takes place. A table of practical uses for the deities is given below, but don't forget to thank the gods both after the work, and again when the result is obtained. They like to be thanked as much as we mortals do, and your magick will be more effective if you remember this.

Godform	Appropriate rites
Ra	Money, good fortune, protection, strength
Osiris	Farming, gardening, law courts, justice, healing of the body
Isis	Healing of the mind, protection (especially of children) gaining magickal knowledge, oracles
Horus	Strength, healing, righting a wrong, protection
Set	To bring rain and/or wind, works of destruction, facing your own negative aspects.
Nephthys	Things of the sea, secrets, protection, aiding the passage through death.
Anubis	Travel, protection, finding lost things, healing oracles
Hathor	Music, dance, love, healing by purging, preventative medicine, protection
Sekhmet	Passion, strength, authority, healing, learning
Ptah	Buildings, plans, arts and crafts, oracles
Thoth	Books, information, science, healing, communication
Asar-Ra	Spiritual development, union with Higher Self If you are unsure of which one to use, meditate on the problem.

THE CLOSE

Just as the circle must be opened at the start, it must be closed at the end, and this is done in a very straightforward manner. The Officers use the banishing pentagrams, and as the Officer of the East says "The rite is ended", he claps his hands together once, loudly.

This book, and others, will help you to discover the Gods of Egypt. Take what you know about a deity, and use it as the basis of a meditation to find out more. You don't really know a deity until you have experienced him or her, and have felt what they have to offer. It may seem that there is much hard work involved in studying the Mysteries - and there is, if you take into consideration a lifetime of study. But if you work at your own pace you will find that the work is not that hard, and the rewards are great.

18. PRACTICAL EGYPTIAN MAGICK

Within this book are chapters giving suggestions for rituals. If you are already an accomplished ritualist you should have no real problems making use of them, especially if you are already familiar with the Egyptian System. If, however, you are relatively new to the Mysteries, then a few things will need to be made clear.

Preparation is an important part of any ritual is the preparation, for unless you are properly prepared you are wasting your time. The work of ritual actually begins the moment you decide to do one: initially, it involves doing the necessary research to construct the rite. Even if you are going to use an already prepared script, like some of the examples in this book, you will need to read them, meditate upon them, and always ALWAYS make sure that you are certain what they are saying. A magician who uses words that he does not understand in a ritual is like a child playing with a loaded gun, and the results can be similar. So do your research, and you should come up with an effective rite.

When designing any ritual, use your goal as a focus and tailor all other aspects of the ritual to it - colours, incense, godforms used, and so on. The idea is that you decide what you want to do - heal someone's broken leg, for example - and then choose the appropriate deity. In this case, you could use one of the healing deities; Isis, Sekhmet, or Thoth, and for a broken leg the best mode of healing is rapid tissue repair, so for this you would use Sekhmet.

Now you have your goal and your deity, the rest should follow naturally. Sekhmet's colour is red, so use red candles on the altar. She is a fire deity, so burn a fire incense. Use an ankh to direct your healing energies, because it is her symbol. The use of aromatic anointing oils can have a profound effect in ritual: if your "patient" is in the circle, anoint him/her with an oil that is normally used for pain relief or bone repair (consult a good text on aromatherapy, and even include a therapeutic massage if your skills are up to it) and then anoint yourself with a magical oil.

For visualisation work, S.H.O.A.R. uses two oils; frankincense on the right temple, clary sage on the left. PLEASE NOTE - PREGNANT WOMEN SHOULD NOT USE CLARY SAGE. The frankincense is calming and stills the mind, and when rubbed into the temple on the right side of the head affects the left hemisphere of the brain and so makes your "logic circuits" less active. Clary sage is a euphoric and will stimulate the more creative right hemisphere of the brain. The combination of these oils helps place you in an ideal state for effective magical visualisation.

The main thing is that every possible aspect of the rite should be directly tied in to the goal of the rite with the use of correspondences. The next thing is to use these things to help train your full concentration on the goal - the better you can focus on your goal the better the results will be. Once you know what you will be doing, run through it a few times without the visualisations or willpower, just as an actor rehearses his part in a play to get it right. If you can, memorise your words, but if the ritual is only going to be performed once this is not essential.

Now we come to the day of the ritual itself, and the preparation of the temple. Clear away all unwanted objects from the temple area, dust and vacuum or sweep out, and finally wash everything down, even the walls, with a good psychic disinfectant such as a weak solution of sea salt or an infusion of borage. Next, set up the altar with a central figure of the deity, be it a statue or a picture. Strictly speaking, all you need is an image of the deity, two altar candles and a cloth of the right colour, but you can add to these the godform's symbol, a symbol connected with the goal, a picture of the person you are doing it for, and so on. The golden rule of altar arrangement is that it should feel right, and that it is symmetrical or at least balanced. If you place an ankh in front of the right candle, then place something in front of the left candle - your incense burner, perhaps. But remember also the silver rule - don't let things get too crowded!

The final part of preparation is the purification of your body, and your state of mind. Whenever possible, you should shower or bathe immediately before putting on your magical robe and entering the temple, to remove all the negative and mundane influences you have picked up during the day: done properly, this will also get you in the right frame of mind. If you are having a shower, set it running warm and stand outside it. See the cascading water as crystal-clear sparkling spring water, part of a natural waterfall. As you step into it, visualise it washing away your cares and troubles. Imagine all the psychic muck going down the drain, leaving you pure. When you feel clean both physically and spiritually, step backwards out of the water, keeping the visualisation going until you turn it off. Rub yourself down with a rough towel, and put your robe on. With a bath, add a few leaves of fresh borage or mint to the water if you can (or scented oil or bath crystals if you cannot), and use a similar visualisation, continuing until you pull the plug out.

One quick note on your robe: it is a symbol of your higher self and so should only be used for ritual. Go to the toilet before you have your shower or bath, and remove the robe as soon as you have finished the rite. The more you wear your robe in ritual, the more it will become energised, so for the sake of that energy don't allow it to come into contact with everyday clothes. Keep it folded and wrapped in a drawer or a cupboard in your temple: wash it separately from your other clothes. Never wear anything under your temple robe (menstruating women are the exception, by decree of Sekhmet). If you want to work outdoors as well, have a separate robe for outdoors that you can wear over clothing if need be.

One part of the opening a magical circle is the summoning of the Watchtowers, or Guardians of the Four Quarters. These are the rulers of the four elements; Air, Fire, Water, and Earth. Do not confuse them with the physical things that share the same name! The elements are types of behaviour into which everything in the universe can be categorised. This is a subtle concept, but once grasped it becomes very simple to use. The elements are governed by the Lords of the Four Quarters, known collectively as the Sons of Horus, as mentioned in the chapter on casting the circle.

Air governs the eastern quarter of the circle. It is symbolised by the dawn, and by a blue disc representing the sky. The element of Air stands for knowledge, communication, spiritual healing and growth. The Guardian of the East in Egyptian magick is Qebhsnuf, pronounced Kweb-Snuff. Fire governs the southern quarter of the circle. It is symbolised by noon, and by a red triangle representing the camp-fire. The element of Fire stands for transformation, change, purification, and energy. The Guardian of the South in Egyptian Magick is Duamutef, pronounced Doo-Amm-Ooh-Teff.

Water governs the western quarter of the circle. It is symbolised by the sunset, and by a green or silver crescent moon, points up, and represents a chalice or receptacle. The element of Water stands for healing, intuition, the emotions, and psychic ability. The Guardian of the West in Egyptian Magick is Imsety, pronounced Imm-Settee.

Earth governs the northern quarter of the circle. It is symbolised by midnight, and by a yellow square representing a field of ripe corn. The element of Earth stands for stability, strength, material things, death and rebirth. The Guardian of the North in Egyptian Magick is Hapi, pronounced Har-Pee.

When using the circle ritual given in this book, the appropriate image should be visualised when summoning the Guardian for each Quarter, as given in the chapter on casting the circle. Give each a background relevant to the element, for example a volcanic background for Duamutef, with the relevant Son of Horus standing in the foreground. The invoking and banishing pentagrams should be practiced so that they can be drawn accurately. Those familiar with the elemental pentagrams may use them, but for the sake of simplicity you can get away with using the invoking and banishing earth pentagram, described below, for all the quarters.

The invoking pentagram starts at the top point. Using your dagger, or the first two fingers of your right hand, draw at arm's length a straight line from a point level with the middle of your forehead to your left hip. The next line is from left hip to right shoulder, then to left shoulder, then to right hip, back to the third eye, and finally repeat the first line to the left hip. Visualise the lines being drawn in shining blue light, hanging in the air once drawn, and see the Son of Horus and his landscape through the centre of the pentagram. The banishing pentagram starts at the left hip and reverses the process: left hip to third eye, to right hip, to left shoulder, to right shoulder, to left hip, to third eye. Practice both pentagrams in front of a mirror, so that you can get them symmetrical and neat before you try to use them in a ritual.

The priests of ancient Egypt did not actually cast circles, but they did work in heavily consecrated purpose-built temples that had been in use for centuries: they also wore an armoury of protective talismans. The circle is the modern equivalent of both of these, and is more effective for the modern mind.   The rite itself can be one of several types. When working for a particular outcome to improve someone's life, the important thing is to focus your attention on the desired outcome. Not, I repeat NOT on how it occurs. Don't see it happening, see it done!

Rites of celebration can be used to recognise an event in someone's life; a wedding, a birth, and so on. Many systems have special rites for these occasions, because they drive the reality of the event into the subconscious minds of both subject and participants. Modern western societies have lost the coming of age ritual, and now pay the price in frustrated youth. Working a ritual enactment of a scene from a legend can also be a celebration, and when these are worked into an annual cycle they can have a profound effect on the participants. The goal here is to experience the event as fully as possible, and to be aware of the resulting effects on your life.

There are three general points common to any type of ritual. The first point is that the simpler the rite is, the easier it is to follow. Because you can follow it better, you can put more energy into it, and so it becomes more powerful. The second point is that you must concentrate totally on what you are doing, and this necessitates training yourself to concentrate properly using various meditation techniques. The better you can concentrate, the more effective your rites will be.

Finally, it is vital that you earth yourself and the working immediately the rite is over. To earth yourself, eat something and get your bare feet in contact with the ground outdoors if possible. The most important thing is to involve your physical body in something mundane: so get your robe off, your ordinary clothes on, and eat something. Traditionally the priesthood of Ancient Egypt would drink hot chocolate after a rite!

To earth the rite when a physical object has been charged, place it on the ground for a while and then put it somewhere safe, somewhere where it won't be found by your dog, your children, or your cleaner. Where external energies have been involved, make an offering of food and/or wine to the relevant deity, and throw it to the ground - in the ancient temples, they had great libating vessels that everyone used, then the poor We'eb priests had to manhandle them outside to return the contents to the earth. It is still a tradition in S.H.O.A.R. that the most junior initiates perform the libations, and while I remind them that they do not have to carry huge stone vessels like the We'ebs of Khem had to, they remind me that the We'ebs seldom got rained on.

19. MAKING RITUAL EQUIPMENT

Most of the major museums of the world have Egyptology sections to which you can go to see the regalia and tools of the Egyptian Priesthood. Wands, sceptres, crowns, offering tables, and libation vessels are all on display, richly decorated, beautifully made, and exquisite to see.

The temples were affluent, and employed the very finest of craftsmen to create their ritual items - no cost was too great for the gods. It would be easy to equate this extravagance with a simple materialistic desire, but these costly treasures were not just for show: each and every item used in the rites of Khem was designed with a specific spiritual function in mind, as well as a symbolic value.

A sceptre, for instance, denoted authority but also operated as a transmitter of psychic energy and will, inset with jewels to amplify the power of the priest's mind in much the same way as a magus wand does today. Another example is the crook carried by the Pharaoh, the Kher Heb Priest, and the god Osiris. It symbolises leadership, but leadership of a type that infers guidance and protection, with close interaction. This leadership is not the same as that symbolised in modern times by the clenched fist.

There is nothing worse than to prepare a beautiful and moving ritual, to rehearse it until it is perfect in your mind, only to have it spoiled by shoddy or makeshift robes, equipment, and regalia. Of course if you are working solo this does not matter - you can forgive anything if it is your own fault - but in a group working appearances can make or break the whole rite.

How can you visualise someone as speaking for Ra when he is in his only robe, a purple one, with a crown that looks like his three-year old daughter made it?

For best results in Egyptian Magick, when you work in a group you should aim for calm, uniformity and quality. If everyone is wearing the same style white robe, they will not only feel and look like they belong as a group, they will be evoking the appearance of the ancient priests of Khem. The perfect Egyptian robe for modern use is a full-length white cotton or linen one, with a simple neckline and elbow-length sleeves. If this is impossible, provided the robes are simple and all of the same style, the effect will be there.

The simplest and most appropriate head-dress to wear is a white nemyss. These are quite easy to make. Measure the distance from the centre of your forehead - where you want the head-band to be - over the top to a point on your spine at about shoulder level (see diagram). Using the measured distance this as a radius, cut out a semi-circle with "wings" as shown. Hem the piece neatly and join it to a headband made of some sort of stiff white interfacing material or stiffened fabric, with a section at the back made of elastic, or velcro, or leave an extra length to tie. And there you have it - your white nemyss. For special occasions you can make nemysses in quarter and godform colours.

Something else you might like to make for special occasions are ritual masks, which are surprisingly easy to make well with a little patience. You will need a helper and a couple of packs of bandage impregnated with plaster-of-paris. At the time of writing, the easiest brand to obtain in the UK is Gypsona, which most local chemists should be able to obtain for you within a couple of days. Ask for the 7.5cm width, or even narrower if you can find an alternative brand. You will also need some vaseline and a basin of lukewarm water.

157

The first step is to make a mold of your face. You will need a partner for this, so work in pairs - with friends this can be a relaxing and meditative experience. Settle your partner down on his/her back on a table or massage bench if possible, on the floor if not. Make sure there are old towels or blankets beneath your partner, and protect their hair with an old headscarf or shower cap, because now things get messy. Cover their entire face liberally with vaseline, making sure that there are no eyebrows, eyelashes, or any other facial hair sticking up. Your partner's eyes will need to be done too, so it's probably best if they are closed.

It is essential to watch out for stray hairs before applying any bandages, or your partner may have to be chiselled out at leisure. If this makes your hackles rise, you can use wet paper towelling instead of vaseline - this is good enough for a single mask, but such a mould has insufficient internal detail to use as a template for making other masks.

First, measure a strip of bandage just long enough to go horizontally below the hairline across the entire width of the face: wet the strip by dipping it into the lukewarm water, then lay it in position and smooth out the surface with your fingers to spread out the plaster. Measure and place a second strip which covers the eyes, allowing a little extra length this time, and try to mold it into the eye cavities without causing discomfort to your partner. Make sure the second strip overlaps the first by a centimetre or so.

Place a third strip across the face, reaching down to the tip of the nose; the forth strip goes across the mouth and curves up a little at the ends towards the ears, following the jaw. Before putting this one in place let your partner know that you are going to cover the mouth, because after this he or she can not talk or even smile until the mask is removed. This is the point to dance around blowing raspberries - but not if you want the mask to look reasonable. If you want a good mask, avoid wisecracks from here on.

The fifth strip is placed under the chin, and then we start to reinforce the mold. Use two vertical strips, one on either side of the nose, remembering to mold them to the features and to spread the plaster well - this determines the finish on the mask. A shorter strip goes from the hairline to the tip of the nose: then a strip folded in half goes over the mouth with the folded edge against the nose, and another strip under the chin. Fold the outward edge of this piece underneath so that it becomes a smooth bottom edge, reducing the need to trim later. Finally, place two strips down the sides of your partner's face, roughly where you want the edge of the mold to be. Check for any apparent weak spots and place additional strips there: then simply wait for five minutes or so to give the plaster a chance to harden.

When it feels solid enough, gently lift it away from the face at the chin, holding it on either side by the edges. Remove it slowly, in case it is a little too wet, or in case some hair is stuck in the plaster. Once it is off, put it to one side and get your partner to sit up, keeping the eyes closed until you have placed tissues into their hands to let them remove vaseline from their eyes. DO NOT FIDDLE WITH THE MASK FOR FORTY-EIGHT HOURS.

The mask can now either be painted as it is, or used as a mold for making a solid face around which more elaborate masks may be made. If you wish to do this, block off the nostrils and most of the back of the mould so that you have a cavity that you can pour plaster mixture into. Allow the blocked-off mask to dry for a week, and then make a mixture of detergent and water, and brush it onto the inside of the mold and allow it to dry. Mix some plaster of paris solution up (work quickly once the water hits the powder!) and pour it into the mold. When the plaster has set, carefully remove the mold and you will have a rough cast of your partner's face: the quality will depend on your ability and your patience - practice will eventually enable you to produce a cast that with a little sharpening up will be good enough to be hung on the wall as a plaque. However your first attempt comes out, it should be good enough to use as a base on which to build a mask. But make sure that you support your mold adequately.

Using modelling clay or plastiscene, alter the features of the cast to resemble the deity you are making a mask for. For example, you could build up a beak around the nose and show falcon cheek markings in subtle relief to form a Horus mask base. Once you are completely happy, coat the base with vaseline and build a mask up in the same way that you did on the real face. For a half mask, leave the mouth uncovered. Once the mask is hard enough, remove it carefully. Trim the edges with scissors to the required shape, then finish them by folding strips of the bandage over the edge to smooth it off. Once the mask is really dry, mark the eye holes and cut them out with a craft knife. It is very important to edge the eye holes with plaster of paris bandage, otherwise you could end up reading a litany with an eyeful of plaster dust. Pierce holes for string or elastic, and your mask is almost ready.

Make up a weak plaster mixture, and dip the mask in it or paint it on. Allow the mask to dry again: this gives the mask a nice smooth finish, which can be painted and varnished to your taste. The cast can be used again and again, but ideally should only be used to make masks for the person who provided the face - so you will need a cast each. A death mask can be made by making a simple full-face mask and spraying it gold without making any eye-holes: this can be done either from a cast or directly from the person's face.

One of the most important parts of the magician's regalia is a symbol which hangs around the neck, called a lamen. This represents either the status of the magician, or the godform he or she is working with for a particular rite. They are quite easy to make well and once again, properly done they can enhance the visual aspect of a group working, as well as having a fundamental magical effect on the wearer. You can make a lamen out of any substance: wood or metal will happily take a magical charge, while plastic or Fimo modelling clay also make excellent lamens, but will not hold a charge so well.

You will find in the appendices a selection of lamen designs. These can be enlarged and used as a template to trace onto a sheet of wood, metal, or plastic. The outline can then be cut around, and the design followed in paint, engraving, embossing or somesuch. If you paint your lamen, remember to apply a few coats of varnish or lacquer, otherwise it will not last and your hard work will have been wasted. If you are using Fimo clay, place a template on your work surface, and mold the different colours on top of it, forming a three-dimensional image. Get some pendant loops from a jewellery supplier and attach them to the back of the lamen: it can then be suspended on a cord or ribbon of appropriate colour. Traditionally your lamens should be kept wrapped in silk of the correct colour or of plain white, and should be consecrated using one of the rites given in the appendices.

If you are working in a group and want to give the group leader - or hierophant of the evening - a "badge of office", the traditional apparel of the Egyptian High Priest was an apron. Using white linen or cotton folded in half, cut out a shape as shown in the diagram in the appendix. Open the material out, and on one half embroider or paint (using fabric paints) on the design in gold. Fold the material together again and edge it with gold binding - you can use binding to make the ties as well. If you wish, the apron can then be stiffened with starch.

A little ingenuity can make even the simplest rite into a spectacular visual treat for its participants, and this dramatic effect is important as it compensates for the initial inexperience of the group. As time goes by the effect will diminish as the regalia becomes familiar, but by then your inner abilities and skills will have grown to such a degree that the use of regalia will have become a comforting habit, but will have ceased to be a necessity.

20. APPLICATIONS

The priesthood of Khem applied their knowledge and skill to many aspects of daily life. In addition to their duties to their deity, they performed rites for the growth of crops, the fertility of women and animals, spells of protection for children and property, and many other things. There were five main forms of magic that they performed, which involved stones or amulets, figures, pictures and formulae, names, and ceremonies. Often they combined elements from some or all of these.

An amulet is an object that is worn for protection, luck, or sometimes for more specific purposes. The word itself derives from the Arabic "to carry". In Egypt, a whole series of specific amulets developed over the centuries - many of which were inscribed with hekau, or "words of power". They were used for both the living and the dead: for example, a model of the heart hieroglyph, Ab, would protect the heart of the deceased from being eaten by the Devourer, and was used in the initiation rites to represent the heart of the candidate.

The scarab was perhaps the most common amulet, being both a symbol of protection and of transformation. It was used to effect a change in a particular situation, or to ward off evil spells. The so-called "Buckle of Isis" is said to represent the female reproductive system, and was also called the "Blood of Isis". It was used to give the wearer a share of the Goddess' power and her access to the astral realms. The Tet, symbol of Osiris, enables the wearer to temporarily (for the duration of the rite) enjoy the status of Khu, or perfect spirit. Just like the Dragon ritual of

Enochian magic, this enables the magician to briefly command forces beyond his present ability, though the usual payment is a few days of total exhaustion.

The pillow (or head-rest) specifically protected the head, and has been used successfully to cure headaches. A more general protection was provided by the vulture amulet, which carried an ankh in each talon. The collar was a very important amulet, as it enabled the initiate to free himself from his swathings (his physical body). The papyrus sceptre amulet provided him with vigour and energy, and the amulet of the soul (a bird with human head, or a winged head) enabled him to fly freely through the magical universe. The ladder represented the ability to rise up to heaven, and carried the protection of Ra and Horus. It is used with the amulet of two fingers of stone.

The Eye of Horus is the most powerful symbol of protection, and promotes spiritual progress. The ankh symbolises life and was much used as a healing amulet.

The Nefer amulet, representing a guitar-like instrument, was a charm for happiness and good luck. It was made of red stone and worn as a pendant.

The serpent's head was also coloured red, and was used to repel snakes. The Menat, a kind of rattle, was used for fertility, happiness, health, and the Sam, a stylised penis, was used to encourage "union".

The Shen represented the sun's orbit, and was used as an amulet of longevity, being the symbol for eternity. The steps were closely linked to Osiris, the "god at the top of the stairs", and were used to enhance authority.

The frog represented resurrection, and on a ring or pendant was a powerful protection as long as the amulet survived, so would the person or object it was associated with.

Egypt was famous for the use magical "ushabti" figures by its magicians. For the dead, ushabti figures were provided to serve him or her in the afterlife, while the living magician used ushabtis to serve him on the astral, and wax figures to control people and other creatures. It was believed that an image of a person, god, or thing contained some of the essence of the thing it represented, and all sacred statues were infused with life by the ceremony of the Opening of the Mouth.

Images were used for love spells, for vengeance, to overcome a foe, and to do jobs for the magician. This practice spread far and wide - even as far as Scotland, whose legendary founder was Princess Scota from Egypt. Magicians would make an image of a person and work rites on the image for both good and evil purposes. They could also make wax crocodiles or other creatures that were then brought to life to fulfil a task. The most famous of all practitioners of this form of magic was Nectanebo, last Pharaoh of Egypt, who used wax figures to fight battles, and who was credited with the invention of chess. Even Alexander the Great was given wax images by Aristotle to help him overcome his enemies.

Just as the wax and stone images were used, the pictures of Egypt were also believed to be imbued with life. Temples were decorated with images of the rites used there in the belief that even if the priests ceased to be, the rites would continue. A god or goddess could be contacted via a pictorial representation. Another form of pictorial magic was to draw a picture of a desired outcome as if it had already occurred. This operated as an aid to visualisation, enabling a group of people to concentrate on one thing with total accord. Coupled with words of power, these images became potent talismans that could work miracles.

But of all the magical forms in Egypt, the name was considered the greatest, and the most sacred. Ra called the manifest universe into existence by uttering his own True Name, and the priests of Khem believed that if they knew the true name of a person or thing they could control it. For that reason the Pharaoh was given several names; his throne name, his Horus name, and his popular name. None but his family and most trusted friends would be permitted to know his true name, given to him at birth.

Magical use of a name usually involved associating it with a deity, like so; "If the name of Osiris grows strong, so shall the name of Neb-Ra". For this reason mystics and magicians would incorporate the name of their patron deity into their own Temple name, in order to enhance their own ability and progress.

The Egyptians believed in reincarnation, but attempted to delay it so that the soul could remain in paradise for as long as possible. To achieve this, they attempted to leave as many "ties" of the old persona behind as they possibly could, in the belief that this prevented a new persona from being established. By embalming the body they prevented rebirth, as the soul could not return to a new body while the old one still existed. By writing the name of the deceased where all could read it, they ensured the continuing existence of the persona of that lifetime. For as they said, while a man's name lives, so lives the man.

For the initiates of the Temple, the true name was not the one given by the parents. The Pharaoh's name at birth was decided upon by the Inner Priesthood, but no great spiritual significance was attached to the name chosen by a mother or father. Although the birth name was guarded carefully, as it was by all Egyptians, the initiate received an outer temple name and a secret name, only to be uttered in the presence of the God. This latter name embodied the essence of what the initiate was and all that he could be, and if an enemy got hold of it he could write it on papyrus and burn it, destroying the initiate.

All magical and religious acts have a degree of ceremony to them, but the temple priests developed their ceremonies to take full advantage of all psychic, psychological, and dramatic effects. The aim of ceremony was to unite the participants in a concentrated focus on one thing - the desired outcome of the rite. Years of training in the art of concentration and visualisation, coupled with knowledge of the hidden meaning of things and the overwhelming atmosphere of the temple created a unity within the group unparalleled by any modern event.

There were four types of ceremony performed by initiates. The first was for the mundane needs of the practitioner; food, riches, love, status, and so on. Next came the rites for higher needs; spiritual evolution, education, and exploration. Thirdly, there were the daily rites of devotion and attendance to the deity that enabled the other rites to be effective, and finally there were the funeral rites performed for the nobility.

Rites for mundane needs - low magic - are well documented, if somewhat ridiculed by scholars. Some of the stranger rites can barely be taken seriously, such as the "Rite for the Ascent of the Uterus" designed to obtain the sexual pleasures of a chosen female, which involves smearing honey and rock-salt on your phallus and making love to her - if you've got that far, you hardly need to use magic!

High magic, for spiritual development, is the main part of the temple initiate's work. The priests would spend much of their time travelling through the realms of the magical universe, exploring and learning as they went. We will come back to this in a moment.

The daily rites for the deities were seen as vital to the temple's existence. The god would be dressed, fed, taken to visit other deities, and put to bed in exactly the way the Pharaoh was treated. This was no brainless idolatry, but had several important purposes. Firstly, the offerings of food and drink supported the priesthood - the essence, or Ka, of the food went to the gods, but its physical substance fed the priests. Treating the statue of the god as a living person encouraged the people to think of the god as a living being among them, which increased the deities - and the temple's - power. Finally, the rites were an act of devotion designed to help the priests "tune-in" to their deity in a very intimate way.

But what about the high magic? The priests and priestesses engaged in spiritual exercises that not only strengthened the effectiveness of their rites, but were designed to produce enlightenment. The most used technique was that of guided meditation, seen as journeying to the astral realms (the pathworkings in this book have been structured to work in this way). Other exercises involved meditating on symbols, words and ideas, much as modern mystics practise transcendental meditation. This was combined with the more mundane lessons on healing and therapy.

Egyptian healing was conducted in a manner quite similar to modern spiritualist practice, though there was often the added element of one of the healers being dressed up as Anubis or Sekhmet for effect. Basically the healer who was doing the actual work would call on the deities and channel the healing energy into the patient. One modern form of healing in this way, as practiced by S.H.O.A.R., is as follows. Seat your patient on an upright chair, and stand behind him. Draw in energy from above and below, placing your palms together as you visualise the energy circulating around you body. Call on the deities in your mind, visualising them as you do so, like this:

"Anubis at my left hand, Horus at my right. Behind me Osiris, above me Mighty Thoth, and before my Third Eye Great Ra." Place your hands gently on the patient's shoulder, calling the goddesses and visualising them as you do so, saying in your mind: "Nephthys at his left foot, Hathor at his right. Behind them stands the blessed Isis, and Sekhmet is all around."

Push energy into the patient from the deities, visualising it as a blue or green light. Change your stance so that you are cupping the patient's head in your hands, with your little fingers touching at his/her throat, and repeat the mental phrases as you visualise the aura of the patient being strengthened and revitalised. Then pass your hands around and down without touching the patient, and walk round to the front. Kneel before the patient, taking both his/her hands in yours. Visualise the energy circulating out of your right hand, up the patient's arm, down one side of the spine, up the other, down the other arm and into your left hand. Let it run up your left arm, across your shoulders, and down your right arm to complete the circuit.

When you have established a firm, regular flow, visualise yourself and the patient rising up through a ring of metallic gold. When you have done this, visualise the gods behind the patient and the goddesses behind you - in their original positions - and allow the energy to leave you at your left shoulder, where it enters the hand of Hathor, and enter you at the right shoulder from the hand of Nephthys. Visualise a cord of green, gold, and blue light from your third eye to that of your patient. In time with the pulse of energy, say in your mind "out with the bad, in with the good, heal, enlighten, and relax" over and over again, until you feel that you have done enough. Then place the patient's hands together, visualising the cycle continuing as you remove yourself from the "circuit". A gentle phrase such as "How does that feel?" will let the patient know that you have finished.

An important thing to note is that you do not merely remove the bad energies, but replace them with energies to promote health. This is because the "hole" will fill up with whatever is available, which is probably more unsuitable energy. Filling it up with good energies eradicates the chance of relapse, and can help lessen the chance of future illnesses. I must stress that spiritual healing should not be used as an alternative to medical treatment except in minor ailments, but rather as an aid to that treatment. Nor should it be given to patients on psycho-active medication, such as anti-depressants, hypnotics and suchlike, because the balance between cure and harm with these drugs is extremely fine and easily upset.

21. FORMING A LODGE

Once you are working with a group, you may want to make things more formal. The first rule of doing this is do not form a formal group until you are sure that everyone can work together without any dissent. Providing this requirement can be met, it is time to elect - the one and only time democracy comes into magick - your Lodge Master, and work together on the structure of the group; how it will operate, where it will meet, etc.

Ultimately, the format you use is up to you, but as a guideline here is the basic set-up of a typical S.H.O.A.R. Lodge. Firstly, there needs to be a minimum of four in the group, preferably five. The one who is elected Master should be the best combination of ability, leadership, enthusiasm and objectivity - electing a "powermonger" is dangerous, as is electing an incompetent. Be prepared to not be elected yourself, and to accept another as Master, even if it was your idea to set the thing up in the first place. There is no room for Ego in magick.

There are four Lodge officers, and although the Master may be one of them, it is better if he or she is separate. The Officer of the East is the celebrant, and is responsible for organising the rituals and mediating the godform. South is the Guardian, protecting from astral and physical intrusion, while West is the scryer, responsible for noting what is happening non-physically during the rite, and writing a report afterwards. North is the Keeper of the Temple, responsible for the physical arrangement, candles, and cleaning - though delegation and sharing is advised when it comes to cleaning!

In a small group it is a good idea to rotate the Officers so that everybody gets a go in each quarter. The Master, if not an Officer, should be able to back-up anyone who needs it, or stand in for absentees on the night. The others should check with the Master for decisions on anything they are unsure of. In a larger group with members at different levels of expertise, it is usual to make the Officer of the East a senior member, and give the other quarters to less experienced members when the work is light, for their own practice and development.

The group should devise a rite of initiation for new members into the group, and should undergo it themselves, one by one, so that the group mind can begin to form. The formation of this rite will take careful study and much meditation, but the work will be rewarded by the experience of your first new member. If you intend to have degrees or grades, base them on a system that you already have training in, or base them on the ten gates as given in this book. Do not initially give yourself an exalted degree, but let the "council of elders" jointly choose each other's degrees, being as objective as possible.

Keep records of all decision-making meetings, with minutes. This may sound boring, but if your group grows it will aid you at a later date to draw up a constitution. The notes will also be of great interest if your group is long-lasting, and future students want to research its roots. Whatever else you do, never give false or misleading stories about your group's origins or you own training - it will always backfire on you as it has backfired on so many others. Should you become prominent in esoteric "circles" there will be enough rumour and scandal about you without you adding to it yourself. At a more basic level, whether your group is intended to be formal or otherwise, try to get together people of roughly equal experience initially - two long-term students and two beginners is not a group, it is a teaching situation which is valid and can work with the right people, but is not usually a good basis for a formal Lodge.

Lastly, S.H.O.A.R. itself will always assist groups in getting started in the Egyptian Mysteries, with help and guidelines. If you feel you would like help with your group, contact them at the address given in the chapter on S.H.O.A.R., or write to the author via the publisher.

It goes without saying that there are several commonsense rules that should be applied to your group. Firstly, do not include anyone under the age of eighteen, or who is not legally responsible for their own life. If you do, you will almost certainly end up with parents, guardians, ministers, or social-workers knocking on your door. No matter how pure and "right-hand-path" you are, someone somewhere will misunderstand and accuse you of subverting, perverting or indoctrinating minors, and that is a criminal offence.

Secondly, don't just accept everyone who comes along - vet them carefully. The best lodge in the world can be destroyed by one wrong person - look what happened to the original Golden Dawn.

Lastly, think very carefully about whether to accept someone with medical problems such as a heart disease, or epilepsy. While they are in no danger from magical practice, and may be well suited to study, if they were to have a heart-attack or fit during a lodge meeting, you can rest assured that some interfering relative will claim that it is the lodge's fault, and that can result in publicity that will finish off your career, your social life, and your lodge. Do not automatically bar people with these problems, but weigh each individual situation up carefully.

22. THE SACRED HERMETIC ORDER OF ASAR-RA

S.H.O.A.R. is a modern Mystery School, founded on the ancient principles of the Egyptian Mysteries. Unlike many such Orders, there is no attempt to demonstrate a chronological succession dating back to Pharaonic times, as no such succession exists. The Order bases its authority on spiritual links with its ancient counterparts, through the entities known as Amenemta and Edfu-Amen-Ankh.

The Order is set up into lodges consisting of small groups of initiates, typically between five and twenty-five members per lodge of various grades and degrees. The Lodge Masters constitute the Grand Lodge, which meets only to discuss matters of policy that affect the entire Order. Each lodge is effectively autonomous in matters other than ritual practice and training requirements.

Training is divided into degrees, from the Threshold degree, through first to seventh degree. Initiation is into four grades of Priesthood. In addition to the regular lodges there is a correspondence lodge specifically formed to run a training program for those unable to participate in the normal way due to isolation or work responsibilities. The correspondence lodge, known as Thoth-Hermes Lodge after the Egyptian and Greek forms of the God of Learning, runs both a postal course for all the degrees and practical workshops to supplement the course and other training programs.

Rituals within the Order are derived from those practiced in the sanctuaries of the ancient Temples, but are adapted for the modern mind, in keeping with our evolutionary state. There are rituals of both "Low" and "High" magick, in addition to rites of celebration and the initiations themselves.

It is interesting to note that in the last few years interest in the Egyptian Mysteries has grown tremendously, and there are many more books available than ever before. These books are from the fields of both archaeology and the Sacred Science, and even a few written from a viewpoint that combines the two. To the solitary pioneering magician a wealth of knowledge is now in print, but the Order offers the chance to study that knowledge in the company of like-minded souls, in an environment of wisdom and with the aid of Inner contacts.

The Sacred Light correspondence course, run by the Thoth-Hermes Lodge of S.H.O.A.R., is a full training course in the Egyptian Mysteries, from basic principles, through Low Magick, to High Magick of the type for which the Egyptian Mysteries are famous. The Threshold Degree Course gives a strong grounding in the basics of Egyptian Magick. It consists of twenty-six lessons divided into nine study packs, ending with an examination for entry to the First degree. Experienced occultists may be credited with some or all of the lessons, but must take the examination to proceed further.

With hard work and applied study, it is possible to do the entire Threshold course in six months, though students may work at their own pace, taking as long as they like. Students doing well in the examination and course work may be invited to accept initiation into the first grade of the Priesthood.

Training material after the Threshold degree includes many subjects particular to the Egyptian Mysteries, such as the Path of Gates (the precursor of the numerical Qabalah) and Sacred Astrology as practiced in the Temple of Hathor at Denderah. If you are interested in the course, or in the Order itself, write to the author, or to the Director of Studies, Thoth-Hermes Lodge, BCM KHEM, London, England, WC1N 3XX. All letters will be answered, and confidentiality will be respected.

APPENDIX 1

The following are designs for the symbols of various deities, that can be used as lamens for students mediating or working with those deities.

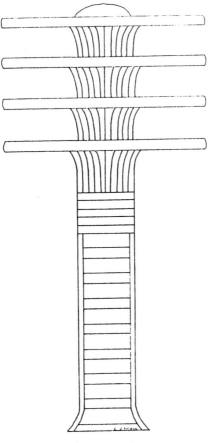

The Tet of Osiris

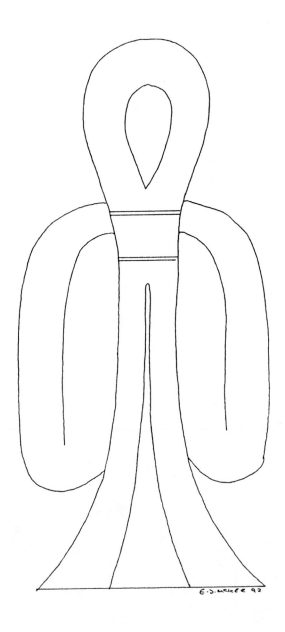

The Knot of Isis

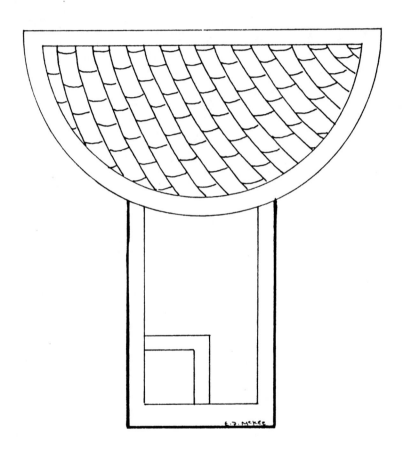

The Basket of Nephthys

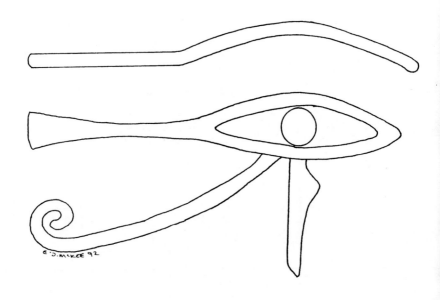

The Eye of Horus

The Creature of Set

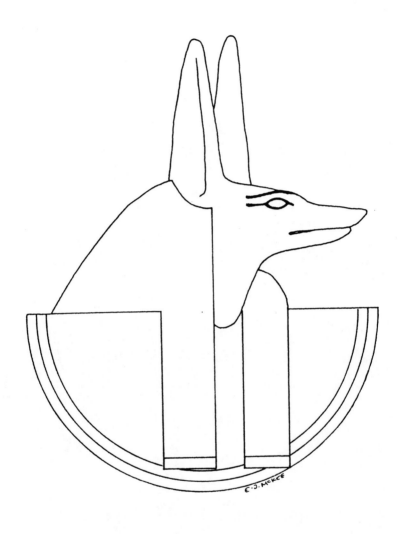

The Gateway of Anubis

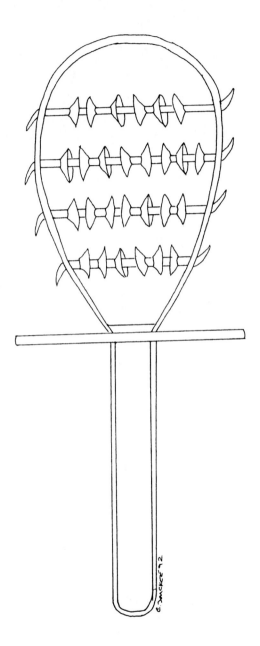

The Sistrum of Hathor

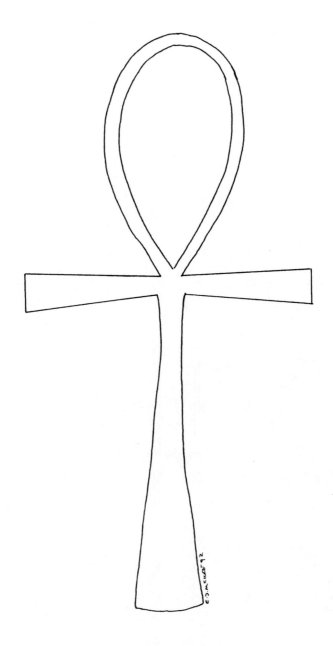

The Ankh of Sekhmet

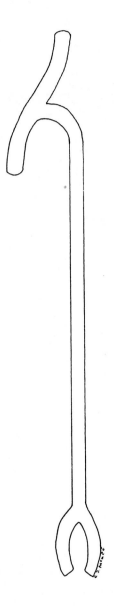

The Sceptre of Ptah

The Ibis of Thoth

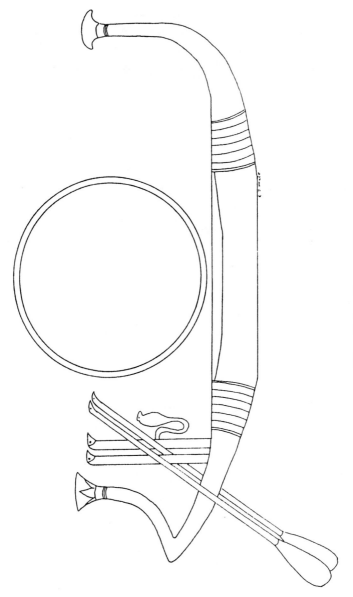

The Solar Boat of Ra

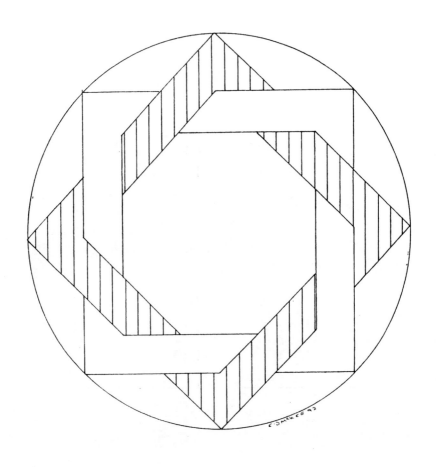

Double Eight Point Star

The Ankh of Asar-Ra

APPENDIX 2

Once a lamen is made, it should be consecrated and dedicated to the relevant deity, and then kept in a cloth of appropriate colour. The consecration should take place within the circle as described in chapter 17.

THE TET

Recite the following while submerging the Tet in water containing rose petals:

> RISE UP, O OSIRIS, FOR THIS IS THY BACKBONE. PLACE THYSELF UPON THY BASE AS I PUT WATER BENEATH THEE, GIVING UNTO THEE THIS TET THAT THOU MAYEST REJOICE THEREIN.

THE SCARAB

Place the lamen in oil of myrrh upon your shrine or altar, and leave it for three days. When the three days are up, visualise energy pouring into the lamen, and say:

> I CALL TO YOU, O THOTH, THE HEARING EAR, WHO LISTENS TO EVERYTHING. I CALL YOU WHO ART DIVINE, AWAKEN UNTO ME, O LORD OF TRUTH!

Then anoint your forehead with the oil, take the lamen and put it on, saying:

I AM THOTH, DISCOVERER AND FOUNDER OF DRUGS AND LETTERS. COME TO ME, YOU UNDER THE EARTH; AROUSE YOURSELF FOR ME, GREAT OSIRIS, THOU OF NUN, THE SUBTERRANEAN. I AM THE FAMOUS HERON, EGG OF IBIS, EGG OF THE FALCON, EGG OF THE AIR-RANGING PHOENIX, HAVING UNDER MY TONGUE THE MUD OF EM, I WEAR THE HIDE OF KEPH. MAY I KNOW WHAT IS IN THE MINDS OF EVERYONE, OF EVERY RACE AND PEOPLE;MAY I KNOW WHAT HAS BEEN AND WHAT SHALL BE; MAY I KNOW THEIR SKILLS, AND THEIR PRACTICES, AND THEIR WORKS, AND THEIR FRIENDS, AND THEIR NAMES, AND THEIR LIVES, EVEN OF THOSE NOW DEAD.THE BUCKLE

Hold the lamen, saying:

THE BLOOD OF ISIS, AND THE STRENGTH OF ISIS, AND THE WORDS OF POWER OF ISIS SHALL BE MIGHTY TO ACT AS POWERS TO PROTECT THIS GREAT AND DIVINE BEING, AND TO GUARD HIM/HER FROM HIM THAT WOULD DO UNTO HIM/HER ANYTHING THAT HE/SHE HOLDETH IN ABOMINATION.

Then dip it into water with rose petals in it.

GENERAL CONSECRATION

Hold the lamen in your hand, visualising light of the appropriate colour around it as you say:

O GREAT (relevant deity), GRANT THY POWER UNTO THIS LAMEN, THAT IN THE WEARING OF

IT I MAY WORK THY WILL. PURIFY IT, AND
CONSECRATE IT, FILLING IT WITH THY LOVE,
AND THY STRENGTH, THAT I MAY BE ONE WITH
THEE.

APPENDIX 3
TABLE OF CORRESPONDENCES

The tables found in the body of the book are placed here for easy reference.

THE EMISSIONS OF THE GOD

GATE	SPHERE	DEGREE TITLE	DEITY
One	Malkuth	Master of the Door	Anubis
Two	Yesod	Master of the Earth	Ptah
Three	Hod	Master of the Hands	Thoth
Four	Netzach	Master of the Temple	Hathor/Sekhmet
Five	Tiphareth	Master of the Pyramid	Horus
Six	Geburah	Master of the Fire	Set & Nephthys
Seven	Chesed	Master of the Words	Osiris & Isis
Eight	Binah	Master of the Water-Course	Geb & Nut
Nine	Chokmah	Master of the Ray of Light	Shu & Tefnut
Ten	Kether	Master of the Universe	Ra/Atum

THE SONS OF HORUS

Name	Pronounced	Element	Quarter	Head	Colour
Qebhsnuf	KWEBS-NUF	Air	East	Hawk	Blue
Duamutef	DOO-AMOO-TEF	Fire	South	Jackal	Red
Imsety	IMM-SETTEE	Water	West	Human	Green
Hapi	HAR-PEE	Earth	North	Baboon	Yellow

APPENDIX 4
BIBLIOGRAPHY

THE GODDESS SEKHMET, Robert Masters, Amity
EGYPTIAN MAGIC, C Jacq, Arris & Phillips
OCCULT ARTS OF ANCIENT EGYPT, B Bromage, Aquarian
EGYPTIAN MYSTERIES, Attrib. Iamblicus, Weiser
THE BOOK OF THE DEAD, Budge, Routledge & Kegan Paul
OSIRIS (2 vols), Budge, Dover
EGYPTIAN MAGIC, Budge, Dover
EGYPTIAN SCRIPTURES INTERPRETED, G Gaskill, Theosophical
DICTIONARY OF EGYPTIAN GODS & GODDESSES, G Hart,
PRACTICAL EGYPTIAN MAGIC, Murry Hope, Aquarian
EGYPT: THE SIRIAN CONNECTION, Murry Hope, Element
AWAKENING OSIRIS, Ellis, Phanes
SPHINX & THE MEGALITHS, John Ivimy, Turnstone
ANCIENT EGYPTIAN COFFIN TEXTS(3 vols), Faulkner, Arris & Phillips
EGYPTIAN MYTHS, G Hart, British Museum
THE GREEK MAGICAL PAPYRAE IN TRANSLATION, Betz, Chicago
COMING INTO THE LIGHT, G & B Scheuler, Llewellyn
THE SPLENDOUR THAT WAS EGYPT, Margaret Murray,
BCAA GUIDE TO RELIGIOUS RITUAL AT ABYDOS, R Davis, Arris & Phillips

Other Titles Published by Capall Bann

A selection of other titles published by Capall Bann. A detailed illustrated catalogue is available on request, SAE or International Postal Coupon appreciated. Titles are available from good bookshops and specialist outlets, or direct from Capall Bann, post free in the UK (send cheque or postal order).

Animals, Mind Body Spirit & Folklore

Angels and Goddesses - Celtic Christianity & Paganism by Michael Howard
Animal Magics by Gordon 'The Toad' Maclellan
Arthur - The Legend Unveiled by C Johnson & E Lung
Auguries and Omens - The Magical Lore of Birds by Yvonne Aburrow
Book of the Veil The by Peter Paddon
Call of the Horned Piper by Nigel Jackson
Cats' Company by Ann Walker
Celtic Lore & Druidic Ritual by Rhiannon Ryall
Compleat Vampyre - The Vampyre Shaman: Werewolves & Witchery by Nigel Jackson
Crystal Clear - A Guide to Quartz Crystal by Jennifer Dent
Earth Dance - A Year of Pagan Rituals by Jan Brodie

Earth Magic by Margaret McArthur
Enchanted Forest - The Magical Lore of Trees by Yvonne Aburrow
Healing Home by Jennifer Dent
In Search of Herne the Hunter by Eric Fitch
Inner Space Workbook - Developing Counselling & Magical Skills Through the Tarot
Living Tarot by Ann Walker
Magical Lore of Animals by Yvonne Aburrow
Magical Lore of Cats by Marion Davies

Magical Lore of Herbs by Marion Davies
Masks of Misrule - The Horned God & His Cult in Europe by Nigel Jackson
Mysteries of the Runes by Michael Howard
Oracle of Geomancy by Nigel Pennick
Patchwork of Magic by Julia Day
Pathworking - A Practical Book of Guided Meditations by Pete Jennings
Pickingill Papers - The Origins of Gardnerian Wicca by Michael Howard
Psychic Animals by Dennis Bardens
Psychic Self Defence - Real Solutions by Jan Brodie

Sacred Grove - The Mysteries of the Forest by Yvonne Aburrow
Sacred Geometry by Nigel Pennick
Sacred Lore of Horses The by Marion Davies
Sacred Ring - Pagan Origins British Folk Festivals & Customs by Michael Howard
Secret Places of the Goddess by Philip Heselton
Taming the Wolf - Full Moon Meditations by Steve Hounslow
West Country Wicca by Rhiannon Ryall
Wildwood King by Philip Kane
Witches of Oz The by Matthew & Julia Phillips

Womens Studies

Menopausal Woman on the Run by Jaki da Costa

Environmental Education

Talking to the Earth by Gordon Maclellan

Capall Bann is owned and run by people actively involved in many of the areas in which we publish. Our list is expanding rapidly so do contact us for details on the latest releases. We guarantee our mailing list will never be released to other companies or organisations.

Capall Bann Publishing, Freshfields, Chieveley, Berks, RG16 8TF.

Latest Titles From Capall Bann. Full catalogue available on request.

Cat's Company - A book of cats and - history - reincarnation - healing - communication - stories
By Ann Walker

Ann explores the role of the cat through history, from being worshipped in Ancient Egypt to being cruelly treated and hated in Medieval Europe. The book includes tales of cats who returned to their owners after death, both in spirit and reincarnated form. Stating that "The Ancient Celts believed that the eyes of a cat were windows through which humans could explore the inner world", we are given an extract from a grimoire giving guidance on how to attune yourself to your cat. Believing in the healing power of cats and our ability to think/talk with them, Ann shares many stories of the cats she has known and loved over the years. A fascinating and enthralling book for cat lovers everywhere.

ISBN 1 898307 32 6   Price £10.95

Psychic Animals - A fascinating investigation of paranormal behaviour
By Dennis Bardens Foreword by David Bellamy

".......remarkably interesting & totally 'different' book on the mysterious powers displayed by animals of all kinds........those who read it will find themselves observing animals, & perhaps themselves too, in an entirely new light." David Bellamy

For centuries animals of all kinds have displayed amazing powers of psychic intelligence as bizarre & inexplicable as the strangest human paranormal experiences. Fascinating accounts of unusual animal behaviour include the stories of the horse that helped police locate the body of a murdered baby, the stowaway dog that sailed 5,000 miles to find his master & the seagull that sought help for an injured woman. In this unique study, internationally known psychic investigator Dennis Bardens presents a persuasive body of evidence revealing & explaining remarkable feats of animal telepathy, precognition & long-distance perception.

ISBN 1 898307 39 3   Price £10.95   210 pages   Illustrated

Psychic Self Defence - Real Solutions By Jan Brodie

How to recognise a psychic attack & how to handle it? This book concentrates on a commonsense approach to problems including interviews describing how people have dealt with attacks. Practical information, based on real experiences, is given on a range of protective & self development measures:- Summoning a guardian. Coping with psychic attack during magical or circle work, Banishing 'evil' influences, Holding your own in the Otherworlds/Astral levels. Protective amulets & talismans, Strengthening the aura, Avoiding the pitfalls on the occult path, Increasing self-confidence in magical work & visualisation, Psychic attack - What it is & What it is not, Elemental Spirits of Nature, Guardian Spirits, the Aura, the Astral Levels, the Psychic Vampire, the Realm of Faerie, Ghosts, Psychic Attack Through Willpower & the Evil Eye.

Price £8.95   ISBN 1 898307 36 9   190 pages   Illustrated

Sacred Geometry - Symbolism and Purpose in Religious Structures
by Nigel Pennick

Geometry underlies the structure of all things - from galaxies to molecules. Despite our separation from the natural world, we human beings are still bounded by the laws of the universe. Each time a geometrical form is created, an expression of this universal oneness is made & from the dawn of time religious structures have expressed this unity in their every detail. In this absorbing history, the first of its kind, the applications of sacred geometry are examined & the full extent of its practise is revealed. Sacred geometry is responsible for the feeling of awe generated by a gothic cathedral & the 'rightness' of a Georgian drawing-room. Sacred Geometry traces the rise & fall of this transcendent art from megalithic stone circles to Art Nouveau & reveals how buildings that conform to its timeless principles mirror the geometry of the cosmos.

ISBN 1 898307 156   Price £9.95   190 pages   Illustrated

The Sacred Ring - The Pagan Origins of British Folk Festivals & Customs
By Michael Howard

The old festivals & folk customs which are still celebrated all over the British Isles each year represent a survival of the ancient concept of a seasonal cycle based on the sacredness of the land & the earth. The progress of the year is marked in folk tradition by customs & festivals, recording the changing seasons. Some events are nominally Christian because the early church adopted many of the practices & beliefs of the pagan religions to supplant them, with little success, demonstrated by the edicts issued as late as the 11th century forbidding the wearing of animal masks & costumes, known as guising, during the Christmas festivities. All over Europe, seasonal customs & folk rituals dating from the earliest times are still celebrated. Some festivals belong to a seasonal pattern of the agricultural cycle, others record the mystical journey of the Sun across the sky, both dating back to pagan religions. Each is a unique happening combining Pagan & Christian symbolism to create seasonal celebrations which can be experienced on many different levels of understanding & enjoyment.

ISBN 1 898307 28 8   Price £9.95   Numerous illustrations   190 pages

In Search of Herne the Hunter   By Eric Fitch

Commences with an introduction to Herne's story, going on to investigates antlers & their symbology in prehistoric religions, with a study of the horned god Cernunnos, the Wild Hunt & its associations with Woden, Herne & the Christian devil & a descriptive chapter on the tradition of dressing up as animals & the wearing & use of antlers in particular. Herne's suicide & its connection with Woden & prehistoric sacrifice is covered, together with the most complete collection of Herne's appearances, plus an investigation into the nature of his hauntings. The final section brings all the strands together, with additional material. Photographs, illustrations & diagrams enhance the authoritative & well researched text. The book also contains appendices covering the 19th century opera on the legend of Herne, Herne & his status in certain esoteric circles & Herne & Paganism/Wicca.

ISBN 1 898307 237   Price £9.95   167 pages   35 b/w illustrations & photos

Crystal Clear - A Guide to Quartz Crystal By Jennifer Dent

This book answers the need for a basic and concise guide to quartz crystal - solving the many confusions and contradictions that exist about this fascinating topic, without being too esoteric or straying too far from the point. Crystals particularly clear quartz crystals, evoke a response, which can not be rationally explained; they inspire a sense of the sacred, of mystery, magic and light. This book explores why crystals are important, their place in history, cleansing, clearing, charging, energising/programming your crystals and techniques for using them for healing. Also included is a chapter on the formation & scientific aspects of quartz which is written in a humourous style to help offset the generally mind-numbing effects of talking physics with non-physicists. Jennifer has worked with crystals for many years, using them for healing & other purposes.

ISBN 1 898307 30 X   Price £7.95   120 pages   Illustrated

Steve Hounsome Meditation Tapes

The Spirit Seeker Tapes contain safe and effective meditations which can be used for personal and spiritual development, to promote greater awareness of the self or simply for relaxation and enjoyment.

Tape 1. Essential Meditations;
a.. Grounding & Connecting b. Tree Meditation

This ideal beginner's tape gives a firm basis for all the other tapes in the series. People who have long had trouble with meditation, grounding and connecting have found it to be of great use.

"I was experiencing terrific stress both physical and mental when I tried this tape. To my surprise, I found myself floating on a sea of healing colours and gained a far deeper understanding of grounding and centering than I had previously experienced. I would recommend it even to those who consider themselves experienced - the calm voice is a great help, even if your mind tends to wander!" Julia Day

Tape 2. The Sanctuary and Meeting Your Guide

Side one contains a guided visualisation which enables you to create and use your own special place or Sanctuary. This can be used as a place to receive healing or as a gateway to a deeper level of meditation.

Side two takes you back to your Sanctuary with the intention to meet your guide. It is necessary to become familiar with your Sanctuary first and the meditation may need to be repeated several times before you come fully into contact with your guide.

Tape 3. The Healing Ring and Purification Breath

Side one is designed to help with self healing. A ring is visualised which passes over the body, removing disease as it passes. It helps those needs of which you are subconsciously aware.

Side two contains a calming energizing and healing meditation. It is ideally suited to those in the process of cleansing themselves, perhaps by changing their diet or giving up smoking. It will also help you become more senstive to the needs of your body.

Tape 4. House Meditation and The Pink Bubble

Side one takes you on a guided journey which takes you to areas which symbolise your Mind, Body and Spirit and also your conscious, subconscious and every day selves. Symbolic items can be moved from one part of yourself to another.

"I found this meditation to be extremely powerful. It not only helps you to understand yourself, but real changes can be made within while following it."

Side two contains a visualisation which can help you to achieve your goals. It also helps you to understand them and how they change. A suitable symbol is visualised, enclosed in a pink bubble and released to the Universe.

"This was also a wonderful way to say goodbye to things that I needed to leave behind me."

Price £6.00 (inc VAT) + £1.00 p&p (within UK) Direct from Capall Bann
Freshfields , Chieveley, Berks, RG16 8TF